Łukasz Jasiński's *The Economics of ObamaCare* offers critical insights into the PPACA to suggest why this latest effort to reform the US healthcare market failed to offer promised results. His analysis adds an essential contribution to understanding the economics of health reform.

Dr. Roberta Herzberg, *Distinguished Senior Fellow, Mercatus Center at George Mason University*

Few Europeans understand how American healthcare works, and the same applies to Americans when it comes to Europe. Yet politicians across both sides of the Atlantic paint the other system as the socialist ideal or a capitalist boogeyman, neither of which are true. Yes, things are complicated, but Łukasz's book is a read for anyone trying to understand the American system.

Zilvinas Silenas, *President, Foundation for Economic Education*

THE ECONOMICS OF OBAMACARE

The Patient Protection and Affordable Care Act (commonly referred to as ObamaCare or PPACA), which was signed into US law in 2010, generated a lot of noise from both supporters and detractors. This book argues that the changes introduced by ObamaCare were, in the long history of government intervention in the US health system, generally not as new or novel as claimed.

The scope of the changes introduced by ObamaCare is very wide and covers, among others: the health insurance industry, pharmaceuticals, employers, employees, or the uninsured. The structure of the book shows the individual causes, key assumptions, and impacts of the reform on individual elements or areas of the US health system. One of the most important aspects of the work is analysis of the phenomenon of the so-called 'death spiral'. The changes introduced by ObamaCare reform make it possible to investigate the causes of this phenomenon on a country-wide scale and enable a broader analysis of its effects.

The book will be of great interest to readers in the economics, management and policy of health and health care.

Łukasz Jasiński is an assistant professor employed at the Faculty of Economics of the Maria Curie-Sklodowska University (Poland, Lublin). In 2021, he completed his doctoral dissertation entitled *Market processes and interventionism in the health system of the United States of America from the view of the Austrian school of economics.* He is also an economist at the Mises Institute of Economic Education (Poland, Wroclaw), where he publishes his original series of essays entitled *On the way to the market health system.* In 2022, on the basis of the decision of the Polish Academy of Sciences (Lublin branch), his book, entitled *Markets vs Public Health Systems: Perspectives from the Austrian School of Economics*, was selected for the best research work for 2021 (Humanities and Social Sciences).

Routledge Focus on Economics and Finance

The fields of economics are constantly expanding and evolving. This growth presents challenges for readers trying to keep up with the latest important insights. Routledge Focus on Economics and Finance presents short books on the latest big topics, linking in with the most cutting-edge economics research.

Individually, each title in the series provides coverage of a key academic topic, whilst collectively the series forms a comprehensive collection across the whole spectrum of economics.

Markets vs Public Health Systems
Perspectives from the Austrian School of Economics
Łukasz Jasiński

Public Policy and the Impact of COVID-19 in Europe
Economic, Political and Social Dimensions
Magdalena Tomala, Maryana Prokop, and Aleksandra Kordonska

Economic Innovations
Creating New Instruments to Improve Economic Life
Beth Webster and Bill Scales

Well-being and Growth in Advanced Economies
The Need to Prioritise Human Development
Maurizio Pugno

The Economics of ObamaCare
Łukasz Jasiński

For more information about this series, please visit: www.routledge.com/Routledge-Focus-on-Economics-and-Finance/book-series/RFEF

The Economics of ObamaCare

Łukasz Jasiński

Routledge
Taylor & Francis Group

LONDON AND NEW YORK

First published 2023
by Routledge
4 Park Square, Milton Park, Abingdon, Oxon OX14 4RN

and by Routledge
605 Third Avenue, New York, NY 10158

Routledge is an imprint of the Taylor & Francis Group, an informa business

British Library Cataloguing-in-Publication Data
A catalogue record for this book is available from the British Library

ISBN: 978-1-032-47227-0 (hbk)
ISBN: 978-1-032-47231-7 (pbk)
ISBN: 978-1-003-38515-8 (ebk)

DOI: 10.4324/9781003385158

Typeset in Times New Roman
by Newgen Publishing UK

To Murray Newton Rothbard: The Most Important
Economist of the Austrian School

Contents

Figures

Tables

Introduction

Any new plans to reform the health system,[1] when announced by individual politicians, attract the attention of the public, the media, and so on. Thus, they can often seem new and different from earlier solutions. One of the purposes of this book is to demonstrate that the changes introduced by the Patient Protection and Affordable Care Act (commonly referred to as ObamaCare or PPACA)[2] were generally nothing new in the long history of government intervention in the US health system, both regarding the newly introduced regulations and their effects.

Naturally, a large range of changes introduced by the new law entailed dealing with numerous further legal and institutional solutions aimed at achieving specific goals. However, a more detailed analysis will show that, in the economic view, they came down to expanding the scope of the ineffective past interventions or allocating additional resources to continue some government programs, for example Medicaid.

As it will be shown, ObamaCare is another series of interventions to tackle problems arising from previous interventions. The new regulations are, therefore, the result of the dynamic nature of interventionism, which means that the willingness to solve specific economic problems by means of successive interventions only worsens the problem by further disrupting market processes.

Applying further interventions is partly based on the conviction that certain problems were market related. This statement would only be justified if there was a real market health system in the USA. Nonetheless, in such circumstances, the state's involvement in health care would have to be limited to a marginal share of public spending (e.g., 5% of public spending and 95% of private

DOI: 10.4324/9781003385158-1

spending) and, more importantly, to direct and indirect non-interference in market processes through government institutions and regulations as is currently the case (e.g., through institutions and regulations such as AMA, FDA, CON, etc.). However, such a situation has not occurred in the USA for over 100 years.

The scope of changes introduced by ObamaCare is wide and includes, among others: the insurance industry, pharmaceuticals, employers, employees, or the uninsured. Therefore, for better clarity, the structure of this book has been arranged as to show the individual causes, key assumptions, and impacts of the reform in relation to individual elements or areas of the American health system.

Notes

1 I am more inclined to use the term 'health system' instead of 'health care', which I explain in more detail in *Markets vs Public Health Systems: Perspectives from the Austrian School of Economics* on pages 44–45. For the purposes of this book, the phrases 'health system' and 'health care' are used interchangeably.
2 For the purposes of this book, the colloquial name of the abovementioned reform or its abbreviation PPACA will be used. The literature also uses an abbreviation for the incomplete name: ACA, which derives from Affordable Care Act.

Reference

Jasiński, Ł. (2022). *Markets vs public health systems: Perspectives from the Austrian School of Economics*. Routledge.

1   Reasons for passing the ObamaCare reform

The increase of costs

Problems related to ever-increasing costs are not a new phenomenon in the US health care system. They have been an integral part for over 100 years. However, one should pay attention to several additional aspects related to this problem. One of them will be the distinction between costs and expenses because (despite some similarities) these terms do not mean the same thing, and yet they are often used interchangeably. The discussion preceding the introduction of ObamaCare had also led to some misunderstandings in this regard.

Rising costs of individual medical services or expenditure on health care often occurred simultaneously. It was related to supply constraints or the expansion of third-party payers, among others. In this regard, ObamaCare did not introduce anything new. The first serious problem with the cost of medical services was experienced already in the 1920s because of the American Medical Association's (AMA) limitation of the number of medical universities and thus the number of doctors. On the other hand, special preferences for Blue Cross Blue Shield health plans and health insurance provided by employers led to reduced direct expenditure and, thus, the rationality of expenditure for medical services. Americans who bore only a fraction of the cost had less and less knowledge of the actual cost of services, and the entry into force of the government's Medicare and Medicaid programs in 1965 only made the problem worse.

Consequently, because of a significant increase in costs and expenses, further attempts to solve the problems using the old methods were undertaken. In the early 1990s, the idea of

DOI: 10.4324/9781003385158-2

introducing universal health insurance for all Americans provided by the federal government – colloquially called HillaryCare – was considered, but ultimately its implementation failed.[1] The proposed assumptions would result in the abolition of private insurance, a restriction of the freedoms of patients and doctors and, in fact, the introduction of a single-payer system.[2] Interestingly, in the heat of clashing political positions, critics of ObamaCare often accused the bill of leading to the socialization of medical treatment in the USA. However, when comparing the changes it made, it can only be considered a more modest version of HillaryCare.

Nonetheless, further attempts to introduce something along the lines of universal insurance were made, this time at the state level. These efforts were finalized in 2006 in Massachusetts, constituting a prelude to ObamaCare. Interestingly, these changes were not initiated by the Democrats, but Senator Mitt Romney associated with the Republican Party. The new regulations imposed the obligation to have insurance in an individual or group form. Employers providing a minimum of 11 job posts were required to insure all their employees, otherwise they risked being fined. In the absence of an individual insurance policy, the employer would be deprived of income tax relief (Pipes, 2008, pp. 36–37).

One of the goals of introducing compulsory insurance was reducing the number of uninsured who accounted for between 8.6% and 11.2% of the state's total population of 6.4 million people. With the introduction of the new law, it was partially achieved. By mid-2008, the number of the insured had increased by around 350,000 people, half of whom enrolled in a free Commonwealth Care program funded by the state government. The real problem, however, turned out to be the underestimation of the cost of its financing – just like in the case of the first years of Medicare. In fiscal year 2007, state spending on Commonwealth Care was $133 million. In turn, in 2008 it was already $647 million, and in 2009 as much as $869 million. By comparison, Senator Romney indicated that these expenses would amount to about $125 million a year. It is also worth noting that these costs would have been even higher had it not been for the fact that not all residents of the state were covered by the policy. For many of them, buying an insurance policy was too expensive and they preferred to pay a penalty for its absence. The penalty increased from $219 in 2007 to $912 in 2008 (Pipes, 2008, pp. 37–38).

There was also a noticeable increase in the amount of insurance premiums after the new law entered into force. In 2007 and 2008, they increased by 8% for individual insurance and 7% and 8% for the family option. It is also worth noting that the state of Massachusetts had already been associated with relatively high health insurance premiums compared to other states. However, this was not the end of the increases. Eventually, in April 2010 the state insurance commission failed to accept as many as 235 out of the 274 premium increases reported/proposed by insurance companies. They ranged between 7–34%, which indicates the continuation or intensification of the trend from 2007–2008 (Whitman, 2010, p. 27).

This is of importance because similar solutions were later used when specifying the principles of ObamaCare. It also demonstrates that any projects of this type remain uncertain as to the maintenance of expenditure at an adequate level. Such a significant increase in expenses was possible because the new insured paid only a fraction of the costs or did not bear them at all, and thus even the relatively high cost for individual medical services did not matter much to them. Such an increase in demand then led to an increase in the cost of medical services. Thus, the effects of the introduction of compulsory insurance in the state of Massachusetts were no different from the effects of the Medicare program launched in 1965.

Public institutions and government programs seeking to maintain costs and spending at an adequate level had often proven unable to achieve this goal in the past. Such conditions led to the consolidation of a system in which an insured American incurs relatively small expenses despite the constantly increasing costs of individual medical services. If most of the costs are borne by the third party, the insured has no reasons to worry. The situation is, therefore, not as dramatic as often presented. It is undeniable that such a system has serious drawbacks, but this does not mean that, for example, every second American does not have access to a doctor, and so on.

Problems arise when someone falls out of this system and for some time is left with the possibility to purchase certain services directly. In such a situation, encountering real prices can be shocking for them, especially when it comes to, for example, hospital services. This makes the society believe in the existence of a *safety net* which protects one from inevitable exposure to high costs in case of falling out. Hence, for many Americans employer-provided insurance plays a crucial role in an employment contract or decision-making process whether (or not) to change a workplace.

The problem of the increasing costs of medical services to a greater extent concerns people who do not have insurance provided by the employer, for example, people running their own businesses, working in smaller companies for which the cost of such insurance is too high, or who simply cannot afford to buy individual insurance. Nonetheless, one can already see some signs of improvement, but not through the insurance market, but because of the increasingly better possibilities of purchasing medical services directly thanks to the development of, among others: doctors offering their services directly (direct primary care), hospitals owned by doctors, or retail clinic chains. An additional problem (hindering the deregulation of the health insurance market) is the question of the insured who already suffer from certain diseases. However, in this case, emotions often obscure the rational judgment of the situation. It is often forgotten that many health problems result from an inadequate lifestyle, not having enough physical exercise, or improper nutrition that causes obesity, and so on. At the same time, the marketization of insurance means granting a greater responsibility for people's own health.

These were among the issues which influenced the proposals for changes in the American health system during the 2008 US presidential election. The proposals by Senator John McCain, the Republican presidential candidate, were to limit state regulations affecting a larger range of health insurances, which was to help lower their prices. Furthermore, McCain advocated abolishing the tax credit for employer-provided health insurance and granting them new benefits for choosing less extensive insurances. According to Senator McCain, this was to increase the role of the consumer. In turn, the Democrat candidate, Senator Barack Obama, was willing to maintain the current financing structure while introducing some changes to facilitate the acquisition of insurance individually and not having it provided by the employer. One of the proposals involved creating a new public insurance program as an alternative to private insurance (KFF (Kaiser Family Foundation), 2008).

Interestingly, both politicians emphasized the role of information technology in the processes of improving the delivery of health care. However, such statements lead to a phenomenon described as a double paradox of technology, which can be observed in discussions about health systems. On the one hand, in the literature on the subject, technology is considered one of the reasons for the increase in health care costs, which undoubtedly affect its availability. On the other hand, it is hoped to reduce these costs, better optimize treatment processes, and so on. These two points of view are mutually exclusive, and the only thing they have in common is that they ignore institutional conditions with too much involvement of third-party payers in financing access to medical services.

Furthermore, the distinction between the costs of individual medical services and the expenditure on those services since is essential because, although often used interchangeably, there are significant differences between them. An increase in the cost of these benefits is not the same as an increase in expenditure on them (e.g., in the form of health care). These costs can be determined, for example, based on the prices of individual services at a given time or by means of the price index of medical services (CPI: medical services), the price index of hospital services (CPI: hospital services), and so on. These costs should not be confused with the costs incurred by the providers of these services. Expenses, on the other hand, are the sum of financial costs (at a given time) that are allocated to these services by consumers, insurance companies, public institutions, or charities. In this case, the expenses of the Americans (households) are not relatively high, but the costs of medical services and the expenses of insurance companies and the government are high indeed. In 2014, household spending on health care accounted for less than 4% of their net income and just over 5% of their total budgetary expenditure (The Pew Charitable Trusts, 2016, p. 4) (Figure 1.1).[3]

Costs and expenses are also affected by government interventions. Artificially limited supply (e.g., of doctors, hospitals, etc.) leads to an increase in the cost of medical services. In this case, consumers (who pay out of their own pocket) may be unwilling to increase their spending. The situation changes only when interventions lead to an artificial stimulation of demand resulting in an increase in spending (already borne by private insurance companies or the government), which also leads to an increase in

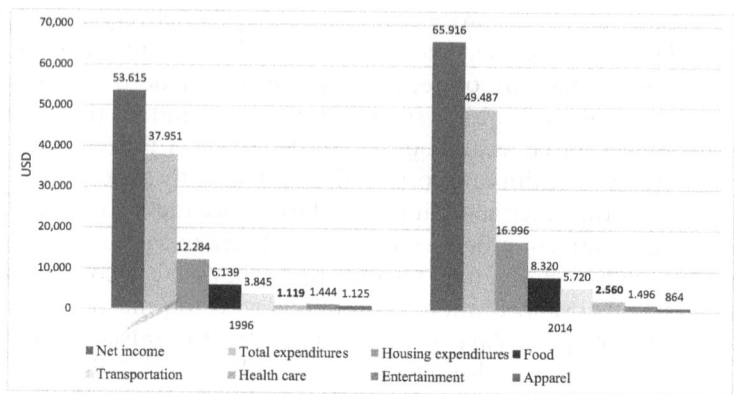

Figure 1.1 Median income and spending structure of US households in 1996 and 2014 for a four-person household (2 adults and 2 children)

Note: Health care expenditure covers direct payments, health insurance premiums, prescription drugs, and expenditure on medical supplies.

Net income is the sum of financial resources (earned by a household in the 12 months prior to the date of the interview) consisting of: after-tax income; income from social benefits (e.g., child support); income from social security, life insurance, sale of securities, pensions, workers' compensation, and other sources.

All dollar amounts have been adjusted for inflation (until 2014) based on the Personal Consumption Expenditure Price Index (PCE) published by the Bureau of Economic Analysis [p. 14].

Source: Own study based on: The Pew Charitable Trusts, 2016, p. 4.

the cost of medical services. It also causes some confusion among the society which does not have to directly feel the rising costs and expenses, but which can hear signals about problems of people who do not have, for example, insurance provided by the employer. In market conditions, the increase in spending is possible due to technological progress and the increase of real wages, but then it is accompanied by a gradual reduction in the cost of medical services. On the other hand, when interventions are used, both expenses and costs increase.

The US example also demonstrates that government interventions were (directly or indirectly) focused more on reducing household spending than reducing the cost of medical services. Also, the official name of ObamaCare, or Patient Protection and Affordable Care Act, includes the word affordable, which was supposed to emphasize the desire to provide access to affordable health by having part of the expenses covered by the government. From a political point of view, this should not be surprising because this approach gave better results – it was immediate, and some American voters felt it directly compared to the gradual decline in the prices of medical services which covered the whole of society. However, such an approach, while politically attractive, could only lead to an extension of old costs and expenses problems.

Moreover, lack of recognition of causal links between costs and expenses may lead to some semantic confusion. It can be illustrated by the Kaiser Family Foundation's (KFF, 2008) analysis of the state of the US health system carried out in October 2008, just before the presidential election. Although the analysis by KFF is valuable and draws attention to many significant problems, it may lead to some misinterpretations. For better clarity of the argument, it is worth quoting a few fragments from this analysis referring mainly to the problem of high (and further increasing) costs and expenses:

Key facts on health care costs:

– Health spending in the United States is an estimated $2.4 trillion in 2008, an average of $7,868 per person
– The share of the economy (GDP) devoted to national health spending has increased from 7.2% in 1970 to an estimated 16.6% in 2008.

The sum of health care expenses and their share in GDP does not say anything on health care costs. It is often pointed out that such a large share of spending, significantly different from other developed countries, is concerning. However, one can also imagine a scenario in which Americans purchase even more medical services thanks to relatively low prices and the share of expenses remains at a similar level. The passage indirectly points to the problem of relatively high costs which result in an increase in the share of expenditure in GDP (KFF, 2008). Nonetheless, it must be emphasized that the indicator is not a cost indicator. Also, the amount of per capita spending may lead to the conclusion that it ruins household budgets, when in fact it is lower than housing, food, and transportation expenses. The following passages also seem to concern the costs:

> Why Health care Is Costly
>
> A variety of factors help explain why **health care costs** are so high and why they grow so rapidly. One factor is expanding wealth. Studies looking at the United States and other economies have found a strong correlation between wealth and **health care spending** – as nations become wealthier, they choose to **spend** more of that wealth on health care.
>
> (KFF, 2008) [emphasis by the author]

It is undeniable that the wealthier Americans become, the more goods and services they can purchase. However, the correlation between wealth and health care spending is not a cause-and-effect relationship. Thus, one can identify countries with a higher or similar GDP per capita to the USA whose health care spending does not reach the same levels as in the USA. For example, in Singapore, which also has a GDP per capita close to the USA, spending on health care in 2014 accounted for only 4.9% of GDP, which was about three times lower than in the USA. Thus, it is not the expenses that are to blame for the rising costs, but the structure of their financing based mainly on the expanded role of third-party payers combined with supply constraints. Chronic diseases are another reason for the rising costs/expenses:

> [Why Health Care Is Costly]
>
> The prevalence of chronic diseases such as diabetes, asthma, and heart disease, coupled with growing ability of the health system to treat the chronically ill, also **contributes to the high and growing levels of health spending**. About 45% of Americans suffer from one or more chronic illnesses, which account for 70% of deaths and about 75% of all health care spending.
>
> (KFF, 2008) [emphasis by the author]

The authors of the analysis, trying to find the reasons for the rising costs, seem to treat costs and expenses interchangeably. It is true that new treatment options for chronic diseases as well as the increasing number of people suffering from them can affect the increase in spending. However, such an increase in expenditure in market conditions is not unusual, as competing suppliers try to provide the services in question in the right quality and at the lowest prices possible. Nonetheless, only under the conditions of consistent state interventionism does the increase in these expenses translate into an increase in the cost of medical services. Another problem is moral hazard. In the light of current regulations also the young and healthy must subsidize the uncontrolled consumption of the services of people with chronic diseases.

Also, tax preferences and a wide range of insurance contribute to the increase in both costs and expenses:

[Why Health Care Is Expensive]

Tax incentives that encourage workers to demand comprehensive health benefits also have been identified as **a factor that increases health costs**. People use more health care when insurance pays a high percentage of the cost. Generally, across the whole population, the share of personal health expenditures paid directly out-of-pocket has fallen from about 40% in 1970 to about 15% in 2006.

(KFF, 2008) [emphasis by the author]

Tax preferences increase the demand for health insurance with an increasing scope. The ability to cover most of the costs of an increasing number of benefits is particularly attractive for people already suffering from certain diseases. The growing consumption of these services through insurance increases the insurance companies' expenses, puts pressure on insurance premiums to increase, and (ultimately) contributes to an increase in the cost of a limited number of medical services that can be provided. The authors of the report aptly point out the decrease in the share of direct expenditure.

The final question worth attention is efficiency:

[Why Health Care Is Expensive]

Inefficiencies in medical care delivery and financing also contribute to the high **cost** of medical care. Studies by the Dartmouth Atlas Working Group and others have shown wide variation across providers in the treatment and **cost** of patients with similar health care needs without comparable differences in outcomes.

(KFF, 2008) [emphasis by the author]

In conclusion, hospitals' monopoly privileges, along with an artificially expanded insurance system, means that medical service providers set inflated prices for their services because they do not have to fear competition and relatively high expenses incurred by patients.

A significant number of the uninsured

Another common prerogative for the introduction of further interventions (including ObamaCare) is a significant number of Americans without health insurance (the uninsured). The problem of many uninsured Americans constitutes one of the key issues touched upon in political and expert debates on changes required in the US health system. It was no different during the presidential campaign of Senator Obama who often emphasized the importance and need to solve this problem. He also continued his narrative as President of the United States (Drobnic Holand, 2009):

> Now, health insurance reform is one of those pillars that we need to build up that new foundation. I don't have to explain to you that nearly 46 million Americans don't have health insurance coverage today. In the wealthiest nation on Earth, 46 million of our fellow citizens have no coverage. They are just vulnerable. If something happens, they go bankrupt, or they don't get the care they need.

The number may seem impressive. Forty-six million people is a much larger number than the population of many countries where the single-payer system is sincerely envied by some American politicians. The number of the uninsured quoted by Obama (45.7 million to be exact) is for 2007 and comes from the US Census Bureau's *Income, Poverty, and Health Insurance Coverage in the United States*. The 45.7 million uninsured correspond to 15.3% of the total US population of 299.1 million in 2007 (DeNavas-Walt et al., 2008, pp. 20, 22). This percentage of the uninsured differs significantly from other developed countries where it amounts to (be it public or private) 0–2% of the population. Against this background, the situation in the USA looks serious. Statements made by politicians and reported by the media, such as the one quoted above, also perpetuate the belief that many Americans are chronically uninsured and, for example, deprived of access to medical services throughout the year. In a country where most people have private health insurance it leads to reflections on the unreliability of the market and the need for further interventions. Therefore, one of the main objectives of ObamaCare in the first place was reducing the number of the uninsured.

However, as it will be demonstrated, the problem of a significant number of uninsured Americans and the serious consequences of this situation has been greatly exaggerated in political debates or media coverage and, in fact, does not reflect the high complexity of this issue. Furthermore, the figures quoted are misleading as to the assessment of the American health system. Since there are many reasons for being uninsured, among others this data should be subjected to a kind of heterogenization. Nonetheless, this does not mean that the problem of uninsured people having trouble gaining access to medical services does not exist at all. On the contrary, there are such people, and the issue should not be underestimated, but their number is not as high as 46 million as quoted by President Obama.

Subsequent fragments of this subsection will also show that in the USA, in addition to issues related to the uninsured, the problems of the overinsured and the underinsured in relation to the insured are also discussed, which in some way is related to the phenomenon of the uninsured.

To perform a clear analysis that adequately shows the essence of the problem of a significant number of uninsured Americans, the following section will be divided into several parts.

Sources of data acquisition on the uninsured

As already mentioned, the data quoted comes from the annual survey conducted by the Census Bureau – Current Population Survey (CPS). There is a section (appendix) devoted to social and economic issues – The Annual Social and Economic Supplement (ASEC) – which contains questions about the possession and the scope of health insurance (private or public) in the previous calendar year. CPS ASEC is not the only study of this type, but its results are widely cited. Importantly, according to the assumptions of the survey, the respondents were considered insured if they had been covered by any insurance for the whole year or its part. In turn, they were assigned the status of the uninsured in a situation where they had not had any insurance at any time during the previous year (DeNavas-Walt et al., 2007, p. 18). Such assumptions, made before the study, overstate the number of the uninsured and, to some extent, make it imprecise because an individual who, for example, has been in the process of changing or looking for a better-paid job for several weeks, is also automatically considered to be uninsured. The authors of the report are aware of these problems and, as they themselves indicated (2007, p. 19):

> Compared with other national surveys, the CPS ASEC's estimate of the number of people without health insurance more closely approximates the number of people who were uninsured at a specific point in time during the year than the number of people uninsured for the entire year.

This factor, among other things, makes these estimates inflated compared to other studies. For example, a survey conducted by the US Department of Health & Human Services (HHS) in 2007 estimated the number of the uninsured (throughout the year) at 39.9 million people instead of 45.7 million as reported in the study by the Census Bureau. In turn, the number of the uninsured in the first half of 2007 amounted to 53.5 million, and at one point of the year it was as big as 70.7 million (Chu & Rhoades, 2009). This shows that estimates of the number of the uninsured can vary considerably, depending on the definition adopted by the researchers conducting a particular study.

Furthermore, the Census Bureau points to other problems occurring while performing the survey that may affect the overstatement of the number of the uninsured. One of them is the survey's retrospective character. It is carried out between February and April of the year in question, but concerns having (or not) insurance in the year preceding the survey. Therefore, the respondents may have had problems answering this question correctly, especially if in the previous year they had been both insured and uninsured depending on the time of the year. They could also have indicated their insurance status at the time of carrying out the survey. Moreover, the study itself focuses more on obtaining income information than having insurance and is carried out at the time of tax settlements – hence the respondents have better knowledge about their income than insurance status. Also, due to the survey's profile, respondents receive less training from the insurance part, which also affects the study's accuracy (DeNavas-Walt et al., 2007, pp. 18, 57).

In the face of the problems described above and critical voices, it was decided to introduce several changes to obtain more precise information on the respondents' insurance status. A survey conducted in 2014, containing information from 2013, included completely new questions that were significantly different from those of previous years. Therefore, when comparing data from 2013 and earlier years, one should consider the significant changes in the questionnaire itself. One of them was the introduction of a new definition of an uninsured considered to be a person who does not have any insurance not at any time of the year, but for the entire (previous) year (Smith & Medalia, 2014, p. 1).

According to a report published in 2014, the number of the uninsured in 2013 (based on revised questions and a new definition of an uninsured person) amounted to 42 million people, which corresponded to about 13.4% of the total US population (Smith & Medalia, 2014, p. 2). However, in the case of this indicator there had been a gradual downward trend already since 2010. In comparison, the same study published in 2013 (data from 2012), thus based on the old questionnaire and the broader definition of an uninsured person, estimated the number of the uninsured at almost 48 million people, which constituted 15.4% of the US population (DeNavas-Walt et al., 2013, p. 23). Therefore, this points out that between 2013 and 2012 the number of the uninsured was reduced by about 6 million. Nonetheless, this difference should not be seen only through the prism of the change of the definition of an uninsured person and the questions contained in the survey.[4]

It is worth noting that the Census Bureau also compiles in its reports data on the uninsured based on another survey – the American Community Survey (ACS). ACS, unlike CPS ASEC, collects data on a larger number of respondents throughout the year – over 2 million compared to about 60,000 in the case of CPS ASEC. However, the ACS adopts the definition of an uninsured

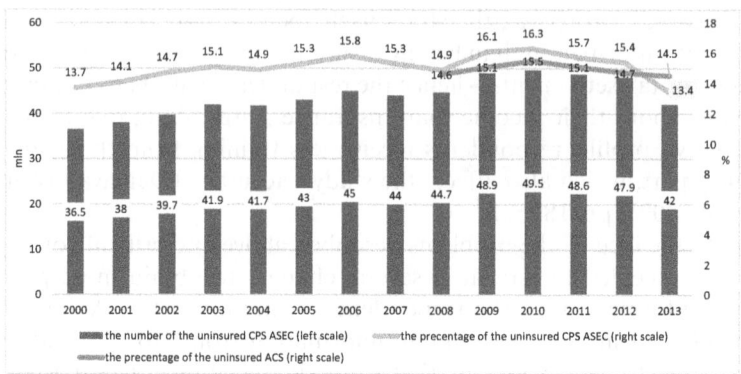

Figure 1.2 Percentage and number of the US population without health insurance between 2000 and 2013

Note: Since 2013, CPS ASEC has included a new set of questions on the insurance status, so data between 2013 and previous years should be compared with caution (data for 2013 are highlighted in a different colour).

Source: Own study based on: DeNavas-Walt et al., 2013, p. 67; Smith & Medalia, 2014, pp. 3–4.

person as someone being uninsured at any time of the year – as CPS ASEC did in 2012 and before (US Census Bureau, 2019; SHADAC/US Census Bureau, 2017). Therefore, the ACS study maintains its definitional and qualitative continuity. In this case, it may be interesting that the share of the uninsured in the US population according to the ACS fell from 14.7% in 2012 to 14.5% in 2013, that is, by 0.2 percentage points. Meanwhile, in the case of CPS ASEC, this difference amounted to 2 percentage points. Thus, the decrease is greater, which suggests that it was caused more by the change in the definition of an uninsured person than by other factors. Data on the number and percentage of the uninsured are shown in Figure 1.2.

Voluntary entry into insurance

One of the reasons for not having health insurance in the USA is, in fact, the lack of compulsion. Leaving aside the question of whether such an obligation would solve problems with access to medical services, it turns out that for some people not having insurance is more beneficial than buying it. There are at least a few reasons for this situation and on the following pages they will be presented in more detail. While this lack of coercion in the eyes of, for example, Europeans may be considered unusual, in the history of the USA it has always been a permanent element of economic life. Naturally, certain institutional conditions, for example, tax preferences, encouraged (and continue to do so) the acquisition of insurance, but even such incentives have not been able to effectively convince the entire US population to buy health insurance.

Moreover, the case of the USA also demonstrates that the lack of insurance does not have to be clearly assessed as pejorative. Since having insurance is voluntary, not having it is also catallactic. Catallactic non-insurance should be considered as a simple analogy to the so-called catallactic unemployment defined by Mises as a deliberate refrain from taking up any work in an unfettered market (Mises, 1998, pp. 595–598). For an unemployed person this situation is more beneficial because they may refrain from deciding to take up any job as soon as possible to, for example, look for a well-paid job or one that will give them adequate level of satisfaction, and so on. The same applies to not having insurance. At the same time, the lack of insurance, just like the lack of work, may also be institutional, that is, it may result from government interventions on the insurance market; then the decision not to have insurance does not bring benefits to the insured as in the first case and is made reluctantly.

Income

What constitutes a significant factor influencing the decision to buy insurance is the person's income. However, the situation in the USA is so interesting and complex that people with relatively higher incomes are not inclined to buy insurance. In this case, the increase in income does not necessarily translate into an increasing percentage of the insured. As Goodman et al. (2004, pp. 218, 220) point out:

> The rise in the number of uninsured occurred throughout the 1990s, a time in which per capita income and wealth, however measured, were rising.

Although it is common to think of the uninsured as having low incomes, many families who lack insurance are solidly middle class (...). And the largest increase in the number of uninsured in recent years has occurred among higher-income families: (...)

- (...) between 1993 and 1999, the number of uninsured increased by 57 percent in households earning between $50,000 to $75,000 and by 114 percent among households earning $75,000 or more.
- By contrast, in households earning less than $50,000 the number of uninsured decreased approximately 2 percent.

(...) The fact that the number of uninsured rose while incomes were rising and that the greatest increase in lack of insurance was among higher-income families suggests that something else is making insurance less attractive.

Furthermore, this trend continued in the following years. For example, the share of uninsured households earning less than $25,000 annually fell from 34% in 1999 to 29% in 2013, and those earning more than $75,000 rose from 16% in 1999 to 22% in 2013 (Figure 1.3). In turn, the share of uninsured households in the total population with incomes from the indicated ranges decreased with the increase in earnings. Nonetheless, even in this case, only among the individuals earning more than $75,000 annually (in 2013) there were more than 7% of the uninsured, which corresponds to over 9 million people after the change in the definition of an uninsured person (Figure 1.4).

The data in Figure 1.3 indicate that households with the lowest incomes, that is, below $25,000 annually in 2013, accounted for about 29% of all the uninsured, that is, 12 million people. Although it is a significant number, it is not a majority. In turn, the number of people with incomes of at least $50,000 annually (a solid middle class), in the same year, accounted for 40% of all the uninsured, which corresponded to more than 17 million people. Therefore, these numbers are larger than those in the lowest income range.

Sally Pipes, of the Pacific Research Institute (PRI), attributes the lack of insurance among people with higher incomes to their

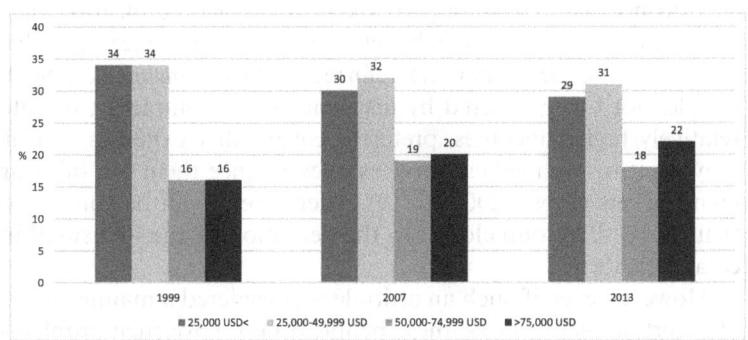

Figure 1.3 Income from uninsured households (%)

Note: The uninsured are people who do not have health insurance for the entire calendar year.

Source: Own study based on: Goodman et al., 2004, p. 219; DeNavas-Walt et al., 2008, p. 22; Smith & Medalia, 2014, p. 9.

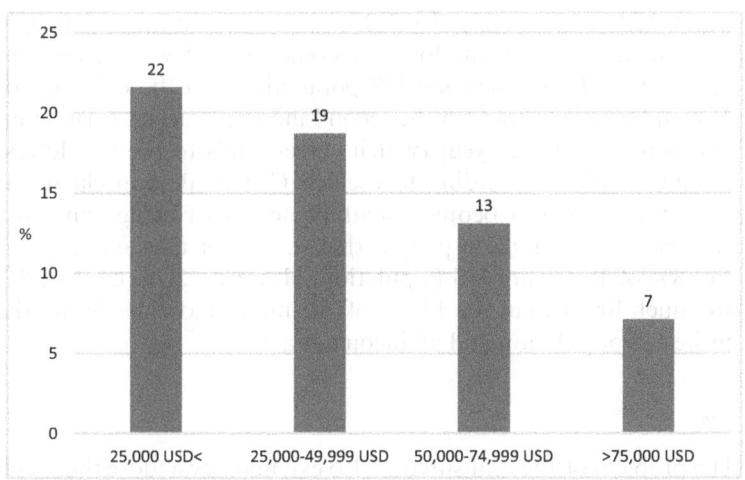

Figure 1.4 Share of uninsured households in individual income brackets in 2013

Note: The uninsured are people who do not have health insurance for the entire calendar year.

Source: Own study based on: Smith & Medalia, 2014, p. 9.

age and lifestyle. Many of these people, being at a relatively young age, do not see it necessary to spend their income on insurance because they are unlikely to benefit from medical services. For this reason, in the USA they are referred to as *the invincibles*. Such people, not being covered by insurance by the employer, despite relatively higher incomes, prefer to cover other expenses, and if they want to use medical services, they finance them out of their own pockets (Pipes, 2008, p. 19). Therefore, it can be concluded that this is the group closest to the definition of the uninsured in catallactic terms.

However, even if such an attitude is considered a manifestation of a certain recklessness, these people do not have such problems with access to medical services as those earning below $25,000 or $50,000 a year. In 2013, the real median income among all households amounted to less than $52,000, which is more than double the upper end of the lowest income range. Also, the median for single-person households was relatively lower and amounted to $31,000 (DeNavas-Walt & Proctor, 2014, p. 6).

In a certain simplification, it can be thus assumed that those who are most at risk of lack of insurance are those with incomes up to $25,000 annually. In 2013, the total number of people without insurance in the lowest income bracket was 12 million, i.e., about 2.9% of the total US population. On the other hand, if including households in the second income bracket, earning up to about $50,000 per year (which corresponds to the two lowest income brackets according to the US Census Bureau classification), the number of people potentially at risk of being uninsured increases to 25.1 million people, that is, 60% of all the uninsured and 8% of the entire US population. However, 2.9% or even 8% are much lower than the 13.4% of the uninsured considering the entire US population and all income brackets.

Age

The problem of the uninsured is also extended by a more thorough analysis of their age. In the USA, the percentage of the uninsured (in individual age ranges) decreases as people approach retirement age (Figure 1.5). For example, the total number of the uninsured aged 19–34 is 15.7 million people (37% of all the uninsured) compared to 11.9 million uninsured aged 45–64 (29% of all the

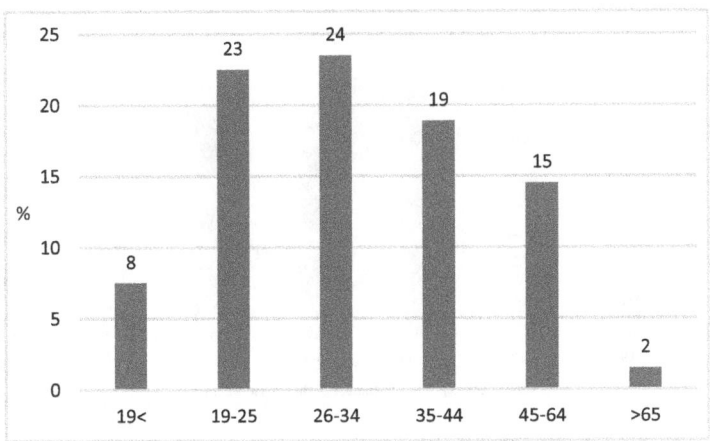

Figure 1.5 The share of the uninsured from different age ranges in the total population of these ranges in 2013

Note: The uninsured are people who do not have health insurance for the entire calendar year.

Source: own study based on: Smith & Medalia, 2014, p. 7.

uninsured). One should also add to it almost 6 million uninsured under the age of 19 (Figure 1.6).

The higher percentage and number of the uninsured from the lower age ranges can be partly explained by the lifestyle or good health enjoyed by relatively younger people. In this case, however, it can be stated that both the income and the age criterion indicate the existence of additional reasons for being uninsured.

Thus, what seems to be of particular importance are state regulations extending the scope of insurance to many routine procedures or the obligation requiring insurance companies to accept all willing employees for insurance regardless of their health condition. This significantly contributes to the increase in premiums, which is most felt by young people with relatively low incomes. In the USA, a young person representing a low health risk cannot purchase health insurance in a narrow scope considering, for example, only the consequences of accidents and rare serious illnesses for a relatively low premium and with a high own deductible. Therefore, such a person cannot get insured against

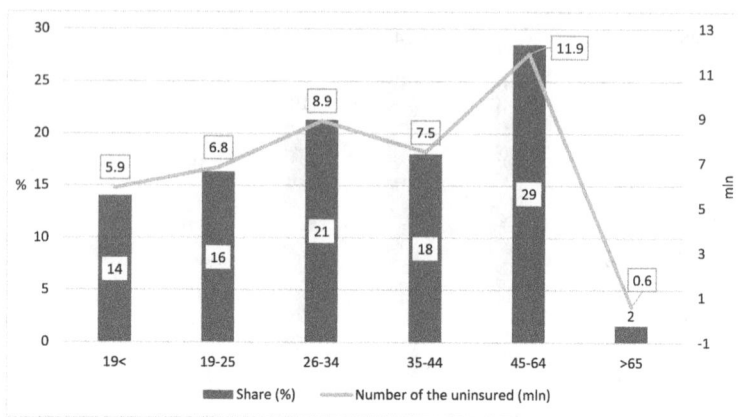

Figure 1.6 The share of individual age ranges in the total number of the uninsured in 2013 and the number of the uninsured in these ranges

Note: The uninsured are people who do not have health insurance for the entire calendar year.

Source: Own study based on: Smith & Medalia, 2014, p. 7.

the so-called catastrophic events. Instead, they have *a choice* of extensive insurance packages that fund many medical services, including routine ones, that should be funded by them (and above all by other insured persons) directly.

Such insurance is more attractive for elderly people with worse health. The lack of an alternative also means that younger people, when buying such insurance, subsidize older insured persons. Therefore, it should not be surprising that some are not willing to buy such a product. For instance, according to Commonwealth Fund estimates, the premium for standard health insurance for a 25-year-old man in New Jersey would amount to $5,580. On the other hand, insurance in Kentucky, which has fewer regulations regarding mandatory medical services, would cost the same person as little as $960 a year (Pipes, 2008, p. 70).

This can be compared to car insurance (comprehensive cover). If such insurance covers breakdowns, road accidents, or thefts, the premium will be relatively low. However, if a routine inspection, oil change, or a guarantee of repairing a vehicle damage occurring before the insurance coverage period (and thus certain events) is added to this scope, then the premium will be much higher.

Therefore, it should be emphasized that in this case the lack of insurance is institutional (and not catallactic – depending on the market), that is, it results from many regulations covering the health insurance market. In other words, the lack of insurance among young people with relatively low incomes, in part, results from overinsurance, that is, from the artificially and constantly expanded scope of insurance coverage exceeding these people's needs.

In turn, the phenomenon of overinsurance is the result of state and federal regulations or tax preferences, which also encourage the expansion of insurance coverage to obtain greater tax reliefs for employees. Such conditions make insurance costs increase. Insurance companies, to be able to maintain the stability of their programs, gradually but consistently transfer an increasing part of the costs to the insured. The increase of direct expenses on insurance (e.g., deductibles) is most felt by households with the lowest incomes. They also do not contribute to lowering the insurance premium, as would be the case in an unfettered market, but to maintaining its level or slowing down the growth dynamics – which makes them even less attractive for the part of the uninsured willing to buy insurance at a lower price.

Interestingly, some institutions view this process as the development of the phenomenon of the so-called underinsurance. For instance, The Commonwealth Fund (2017) defines this phenomenon as a situation in which:

> People who are underinsured have high deductibles and high out-of-pocket expenses relative to their income. For lower-income families, this means spending 5 percent or more of income on health care, while for higher-income families it means spending 10 percent or more.

The institution believes the development of this phenomenon is due to the increasing number of the insured covered by their own deductible as well as its growing amount. According to the data quoted, in 2003 40% of people with private insurance (provided by their employer or individual) did not have their own deductibles in their health plans, while in 2016 the percentage of such people fell to 22%. Moreover, in 2003 only 1% of the privately insured were covered by an own share of $3,000 or more. In turn, in 2016 the share of such people increased to 13%. The Commonwealth Fund (2017) also points out that the increasing level of deductible is making it increasingly difficult for insured people to pay their medical bills.

Nonetheless, such actions of insurance companies are not unusual. They are a long-term result of constantly expanding regulations that significantly hinder the smooth operation of the insurance market. The expansion of regulations leads to the phenomenon of overinsurance. Overinsurance, in turn, results in increasing premiums. This causes a loss of some of the young and healthy insured, a smaller number of employers (mainly smaller companies) offering health insurance to their employees, and so on, leading to an increase in the number of the uninsured. In such conditions, insurance companies and employers begin to transfer increasingly higher costs to employees, which results, among other things, in an increasing amount of premiums and deductibles. Such actions, however, provide some stability for other insured people – without them, their premiums would grow even faster.

Paradoxically, in the situation of a wide range of health insurance in the USA, The Commonwealth Fund complains about underinsurance. Underinsurance could be discussed when an insured person states that they have insured themselves against not wide enough scope of risk in the insurance coverage, for example, only against the consequences of unfortunate accidents, without including selected serious illnesses. Meanwhile, according to The Commonwealth Fund, any situation in which households spend more than 5% or 10% of their annual income on medical services is undesirable. However, the USA considers its problems with the health system to result from persistent efforts to consistently marginalize the role of direct payments.

Citizenship

President Obama in his speech drew attention to the significant number of uninsured Americans – almost 46 million people in 2007. However, the issue of lack of insurance also applies to immigrants, that is, people who are not American citizens. The problem is that by quoting data on the number of the uninsured from particular sources, such as, for example, a report published by the Census Bureau, politicians tend to misinterpret them and inflate the number of uninsured Americans. According to the Census Bureau, the number of uninsured non-Americans (in 2007) amounted to 9.7 million people, which corresponds to 3.2% of the total US population and 21.3% of all the uninsured (DeNavas-Walt et al., 2008, p. 22). This means that approximately one in five uninsured US residents is not American. Thus, the number of uninsured Americans drops to 35.9 million, which is equivalent to 12% of the total US population. Nonetheless, it should be emphasized that immigrants also need access to medical services and that the problem of lack of insurance affects them as much as uninsured Americans.

Furthermore, the group of immigrants, including the uninsured, is not homogeneous. It consists of documented immigrants, that is, legally residing in the USA, and undocumented immigrants.

The first subgroup of the immigrants is the so-called Lawful Permanent Residents (LPR) or green card holders. Such people are legally authorized to permanently reside in the USA. If they earn a low income, they can enrol in the Medicaid and CHIP programs[5] which are subject to certain eligibility requirements. According to the regulations, legal immigrants must obtain qualified immigration status to be covered by these government programs. Most of them must wait 5 years to be able to sign up. However, some states apply more liberal laws in this regard, for example, in 24 states, the requirement for a 5-year waiting period has been abolished in relation to children and pregnant women. In turn, the other subgroup (undocumented immigrants) is not allowed to participate in Medicaid or CHIP (KFF, 2019).

According to the research conducted by Passel and Cohn (2008), in 2007 the number of undocumented immigrants in the USA amounted to 12.4 million people (in 2000 it was 8.4 million). Their research was based on a Census Bureau report which, according to the authors, may underestimate the numbers due to the lack of questions about immigration status. In turn, the data published by the US Department of Homeland Security report 12.8 million documented (legal) immigrants (Rytnia/ US Department of Homeland Security, 2008). On this basis, with some simplification, it can be concluded that the share of these two subgroups in the total number of non-Americans is 50/50.

On the other hand, clear disproportions appear already in the context of the status of their insurance. According to the Pew Research Center, 59% of adult undocumented immigrants were uninsured throughout 2007, a percentage more than double that of legal immigrants. Among their children with the same status, the percentage was 45%, and among children already born in the USA, 25%. This is because immigrant children born in the USA (according to the law) automatically become American citizens. Therefore, they can be qualified, for example, for the CHIP program. This leads to a situation in which some family members are covered by insurance, and some remain uninsured. In the case of adults, it is troublesome due to the relatively low income obtained. The median household income among undocumented immigrants in 2007 amounted to about $37,000, which is well below the national median of $50,000. This is also significant because their earnings do not increase as much over the years, as opposed to legal immigrants (Pew Research Center, 2009).

These data also confirm that the income criterion is one of the most accurate indicators measuring the percentage of the uninsured who may be particularly vulnerable in the absence of insurance. In addition, in the context of the existing immigration regulations (regarding the possibility of obtaining insurance), the number and percentage of the uninsured are overstated in the sense that they include people who, for legal reasons, cannot be included anyway with regard to, for example, Medicaid or CHIP.

Eligibility for Medicaid or CHIP

The last point worth mentioning is the possibility of covering people with relatively low income with government insurance programs, especially Medicaid and CHIP. In this case, one should (again) refer to the report of the Census Bureau. As already emphasized, there were several reasons for the data on the number of the uninsured being inflated. This problem also affected people insured through government programs and those eligible for them, as the CPS ASEC study underestimated the number of people covered by Medicare, Medicaid, or CHIP programs. This was because some of the respondents were not aware that they were covered by such insurance if, for example, they had not recently used medical services. This is particularly true of Medicaid (DeNavas-Walt et al., 2007, p. 67).

According to Keith Hennessey (2009), an economist at Stanford University and former economic policy adviser to President George W. Bush, approximately 6.4 million people insured under Medicaid or CHIP (in 2007) were mistakenly considered uninsured. This could be due to both giving incorrect answers and the respondents' deliberate actions. Furthermore, an additional 4.3 million people were eligible for Medicaid or CHIP coverage but did not take appropriate action in this direction. However, they can still use the services of hospital emergency departments when such a need arises. This obligation was imposed on hospitals with the entry into force (in 1986) of the federal Emergency Medical Treatment and Labor Act (EMTALA), which requires that every person presenting in the emergency department has access to medical services and treatment, regardless of their insurance status or ability to pay (American College of Emergency Physicians, n. d.). This is one of the reasons why the uninsured may not feel as much pressure to enrol in Medicaid, along with a certain reluctance to devote time to, in their opinion, unnecessary formalities.

In total, this amounts to 10.7 million people who are insured or eligible for selected government programs. At this point, however, it should be noted that the 4.3 million uninsured[6] who may be covered by Medicaid or CHIP is a more technical than economical solution to the problem. If they were included in Medicaid, one would expect a potential increase in medical services consumption, and thus an increase in states spending on Medicaid. It could also turn out that some states would have to increase taxes, get into additional debt, or ask for more support from the federal authorities. In this case, the biggest problem is that the Medicaid program itself suffers from many defects such as: dissatisfaction of doctors, low reimbursement rates, a significant increase in spending over the years, or people with low income addiction from government aid. Therefore, the quality of services provided is not the best either. The inclusion of several million people would make the situation even worse. One can even state that the reluctance of some of the uninsured to enrol in this program is caused by its ineffectiveness. It should also constitute a warning against the political tendencies to have an increasing part of society covered by insurance. Anyone proposing such a solution should first answer the question of why several million Americans did not sign up for government insurance despite meeting the required criteria.

Conclusion

Based on the analysis presented above, it can be concluded that the number of Americans or, more broadly, residents of the USA for whom the lack of insurance may have unpleasant consequences, is several times lower than the 46 million that President Obama spoke about. One can take as a certain point of reference, for example, the people in the lowest or the two lowest income ranges, that is, earning up to $25,000 or up to $50,000 annually. In this case, the percentage of uninsured US residents (in 2007) amounted to 2.9% or 6.1% respectively, and not 15.3% of the total US population.

It is also worth mentioning the analysis conducted by Hennessey. Based on the research by the Department of Health and Human Services in 2005, Hennesey identified individual subgroups of the uninsured and estimated their numbers in 2007. In this case, the total of 45.7 million uninsured consists of: 6.4 million people insured with Medicaid but included in the CPS ASEC study as uninsured; 4.3 million Americans eligible for Medicaid/CHIP but knowingly remaining uninsured; 9.3 million non-Americans; 10.1 million people whose income is 300% or more above the federal poverty level (FPL); 5 million people aged 18–34 without children. The remaining 10.6 million uninsured are Americans who are not in the age range of 18–34 years old, who have incomes below 300% of the FPL which still does not allow them to qualify for subsidized government insurance (Hennessey, 2009) (Figure 1.7).

The final subgroup mentioned can be considered the Americans most suffering due to lack of insurance. A total of 10.6 million corresponds to 3.5% of the US population and 23% of all the uninsured. It can also be said that this value is, in fact, even lower because it is based on the definition of lack of insurance at any time of the year and not throughout the whole calendar year. However, in this case it is necessary to consider several million immigrants who, regardless of their status, also remain chronically uninsured. Nonetheless, even considering their total number – 9.3 million – the share of the uninsured in the entire US population would amount to 6.6% and not over 15%. Despite different

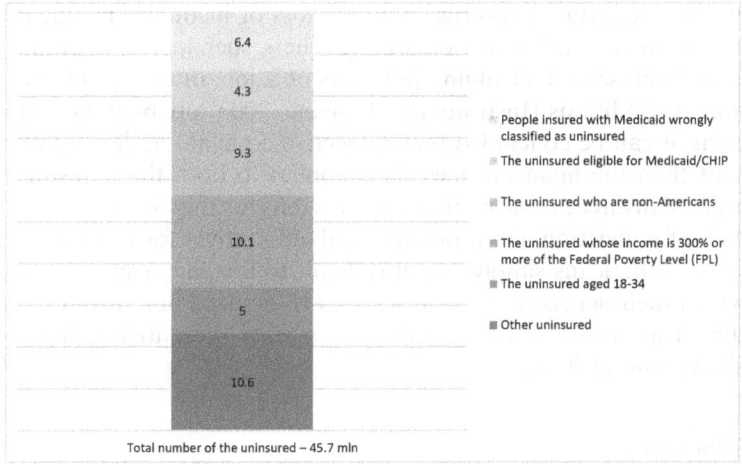

Total number of the uninsured – 45.7 mln

Figure 1.7 The number (in mln) and structure of the uninsured in 2007

Source: Own study based on: Hennessey, 2009.

Note: The individual subgroups of the uninsured do not overlap. The estimates are based on a 2005 study conducted by the US Department of Health and Human Services.

approaches in estimating the rational number of the uninsured, one thing is certain – the data quoted by politicians, or the media, are overstated.

One can also get the impression that discussions on this subject focus mainly on the number or percentage of the uninsured and the undesirable financial consequences of this situation. Meanwhile, considerations on this subject should also be complemented with non-financial issues. The Committee on the Consequences of Uninsurance, based on an early twenty-first-century study, draws attention to the fact that the main problem associated with the lack of insurance is not the financial consequences but the hidden costs in the form of worse health of the uninsured, including mental health. People with no insurance experience, for example, are stressed because of the uncertainty as to the possibility of covering the costs of medical services, for example, in the event of illness of one of the family members. Interestingly, the authors of the report also indicate that the problem of this kind of hidden costs also applies to households with insurance. Such families also experience certain concerns about the loss of insurance by one or all their members because of, among others, such factors as graduating from school, changing jobs, loss of a job, or change of economic conditions (Institute of Medicine, 2003, pp. 6–7). On this basis, it can be concluded that subjective costs are no less significant than the financial ones. This applies to both the uninsured and the insured. In turn, one of the reasons for this situation is the lack of conviction about possible real alternatives for insurance – many Americans simply find it difficult to imagine a situation in which their access to medical services is financed in a form other than insurance. Fortunately, emerging market alternatives can help change this attitude.

Other causes

A study conducted in 2000 by the World Health Organization (WHO), which assessed health systems in 191 countries based on several criteria, also had some impact on the proposals for the changes to be introduced in the American health system contained in ObamaCare. In the WHO report entitled *The World Health Report 2000: Health Systems: Improving Performance*, the USA ranked 37th. Such a remote place among other developed countries intensified voices in the USA calling for further interventions and changes. The report of such a prestigious institution as the WHO was, therefore, evidence of the need for further reforms. It may have seemed that the situation was serious, especially for the country with the highest level of health care spending in the world.

Meanwhile, a closer analysis of the WHO report showed that it needed to be thoroughly changed. As Atlas (2011) points out, the WHO report is:

(…) a profoundly deceptive document that is only marginally a measure of health-care performance at all. The report's true achievement was to rank countries according to their alignment with a specific political and economic ideal – socialized medicine – and then claim it was an objective measure of "quality".

WHO researchers divided aspects of health care into subjective categories and tailored the definitions to suit their political aims. They allowed fundamental flaws in methodology, large margins of error in data, and overt bias in data analysis, and then offered conclusions despite enormous gaps in the data they did have. The flaws in the report's approach, flaws that thoroughly undermine the legitimacy of the WHO rankings, have been repeatedly exposed in peer-reviewed literature by academic experts who have examined the study in detail. (...)

This object lesson in the ideological misuse of politicized statistics should serve as a cautionary tale for all policymakers and all lay people who are inclined to accept on faith the results reported in studies by prestigious international bodies.

To compile the ranking, the WHO used five criteria (divided into three categories) of a certain weight, whose sum allowed to determine the so-called general overall attainment of the health system in the countries studied. These criteria and their weighting are shown in Table 1.1.

However, the choice of the criteria and the results obtained do not provide sufficient knowledge of the functioning and efficiency of national health systems because the focus was placed on issues not related to efficiency, economics, and management but promoting

Table 1.1 Categories, criteria, and their weighting determining the general system achievement indicator

Category	Weight	Criteria	Partial weight
A Health (disability-adjusted life expectancy)	50%	Overall or average	25%
		Distribution or equality	25%
B Responsiveness	25%	Overall or average	12.5%
		Distribution or equality	12.5%
C Fair financial contribution	25%	Distribution or equality	25%

Source: Own study based on: World Health Organization, 2000, p. 39.

more general and difficult-to-measure criteria of fairness, equality, or respect. For instance, category B (Responsiveness) is defined based on two components: respect for the person (50%) and customer orientation (50%). Respect for the person consists of respect for dignity (16.7%), confidentiality (16.7%), and independence (16.7%). In turn, customer orientation is determined by quick service (attention) (20%), the quality of facilities (15%), access to social support networks (10%), and the choice of provider (5%). Moreover, the individual components and their weights were created based on the subjective opinions of respondents, half of whom are WHO employees (World Health Organization, 2000, p. 32).

Another question concerns life expectancy or infant mortality in the USA. These indicators are influenced by factors unrelated to the US health system such as accidents, lifestyle (including addictions), or ethnicity. In the case of infant mortality rates, research methods affecting the accuracy of studies or the definition of infant death, which significantly differ from other countries, are also significant. In terms of life expectancy at birth, the USA ranked 24th. However, this does not mean that the full responsibility for this result falls on the health system.

The dubious reliability of the ranking is also evidenced by other countries in the general classification. At the top of the ranking (and far ahead of the USA) were: San Marino (3rd), Andorra (4th), Malta (5th), and Oman (8th). Perhaps due to the relatively small population and territory, these countries score more easily in the WHO ranking. However, these are not destinations for American medical tourists nor examples of global determinants in the quality and efficiency of medical treatment. Equally high positions were occupied by countries from the south of Europe characterized by more centralized systems, for example, Italy (2nd) or Spain (7th). Surprisingly, these countries have a reputation for relatively poor accessibility to medical services. Other countries that scored higher in the ranking than the USA were the United Kingdom (18th) and Sweden (23rd), that is, countries having permanent problems providing access to medical services[7] to their citizens despite higher expenditure on health care than Italy and Spain. The first place went to France, that is, another country with a highly regulated and expensive single-payer system (World Health Organization, 2000, pp. 152–155).

Such high ranks of countries with centralized single-payer systems should not be surprising given the criteria adopted by the WHO. For instance, such countries could count on better results in the last criterion – the fairness of the financing system. According to the WHO, a fair funding system is based on the ability to pay rather than the health risks posed and encompasses the entire population.

One may conclude that out-of-pocket payments are undesirable in relation to taxes, social security contributions, or premiums for voluntary health insurance. Therefore, the WHO points out that this justice is served more by progressive prepayment than by direct payments (World Health Organization, 2000, p. 35). Hence, higher-income households should contribute proportionately more to the financing of such a system.

In other words, the WHO report was at best based on secondary factors with little effect on quality and performance. This study, being more focused on determining norms based on imprecise criteria, contributes even less to the understanding of the functioning of national health systems. It also ignores the specific conditions occurring in given countries, trying, in fact, to reduce them to normative parameters. For more information about the report errors, see Table 1.2.

Table 1.2 Selected errors of the WHO report – *The World Health Report 2000: Health Systems: Improving Performance* (2000)

Aim
The report was not intended to assess systems in individual countries, but to set certain standards. Therefore, it did not help in better understanding of the problems resulting from the expansion of interventionism.

Low focus on health system quality and efficiency (1)
The report rewarded systems with greater centralization and redistribution in advance, which was normatively considered a synonym for *quality*. It also led to countries having problems with ensuring adequate access to medical services scoring higher in the ranking.

Low focus on health system quality and efficiency (2)
The WHO gave too much importance to factors focusing mainly on the evaluation of abstract criteria of equality and fairness. Health distribution, response distribution, and fairness distribution combined accounted for as much as 62.5% of the total score.

(*Continued*)

Table 1.2 (Continued)

Unreliable data sources (1)
The results in categories B (System Responsiveness) and C (Fairness of the Funding System) were based on the respondents' subjective views on the discrimination of particular groups against the overall population and their numbers. On the other hand, another study involving 1,000 respondents gathered their opinions on the relative importance of individual criteria in the index, which was eventually used to calculate the overall score. Thus, it was a typically normative approach and not an objective one.

Unreliable data sources (2)
The subjective opinions of the so-called respondents were, therefore, of key importance when assessing individual criteria. However, from the point of view of the study, the WHO did not provide relevant information about the respondents nor the way they were selected. Other sources than the WHO report that half of them were WHO employees, and some were invited to participate in the study having entered the WHO website.

No reference to independent studies
Another problem is the sources the report is based on. Among the 32 references to the methodology, as many as 26 are other WHO sources which did not go through the independent review process, and only two publications were prepared by non-authors of the WHO 2000 report. Therefore, to a large extent, WHO referred to its own research without having it verified by independent institutions or researchers.

Unreliable results
According to an article published in the prestigious journal "The Lancet" by Musgrove, formerly one of the co-authors of the WHO study, the results of the report are false. He justifies his position by the fact that, according to his estimates, the WHO's overall achievement index was based on complete data from only 35 out of 191 countries. Musgrove points out that the WHO only had data from: 56 countries on the health distribution criterion, 30 countries on category B (system responsiveness) and only 21 countries on category C (fairness of the financing system). Based on this limited data, however, they created a ranking for 191 countries. Furthermore, the results for some countries were estimated based on data from, e.g., their individual regions and not the whole country's area.

Results
Despite so many evident mistakes and dubious results, the WHO report served as another argument for introducing further changes in the US health system, including the introduction of ObamaCare. However, it did not have a solid scientific basis to be considered reliable.

Source: Own study based on: Atlas, 2011.

Notes

1 The name derives from Hillary Clinton from the Democratic Party and the wife of contemporary American president, Bill Clinton.
2 More on the criticism of HillaryCare in: Rothbard (2006, pp. 127–133).
3 Interestingly, the share of health care spending in total household expenses was at a similar level in the past, which should not be surprising given the growing popularity of private insurance and the Medicare and Medicaid programs' entry into force. This share amounted for, respectively: 4.7% (1917–1919), 5.1% (1950), 6.6% (1960–1961), 4.7% (1972–1973) and 4% (1986–1987).
4 Although the number is close to the difference of 5.8 million between the number of the uninsured reported by the Census Bureau (CPS ASEC) in 2007 (45.7 million) and the number of the uninsured in the same year published by the Department of Health and Human Services (39.9 million).
5 Moreover, after the entry into force of ObamaCare, they can buy insurance using the so-called insurance exchanges and they have the right to subsidize their premiums in these insurances.
6 Interestingly, earlier studies speak of even larger numbers. For example, a 2003 report by the Blue Cross Blue Shield Association mentions about 14 million uninsured Americans who have the option to enrol in Medicaid or CHIP. However, such a significant number is largely due to basing estimates on a Census Bureau report inflating the total number of the uninsured and, at the same time, understating the number of the insured under Medicaid/CHIP. See more: Blue Cross Blue Shield Association, 2003.
7 In this context, it is worth analysing the annual EuroHealth Consumer Index reports in which these countries achieve relatively poor results when it comes to access to medical services.

References

American College of Emergency Physicians (n. d.). EMTALA Fact Sheet, www.acep.org/life-as-a-physician/ethics--legal/emtala/emtala-fact-sheet/ (accessed: 25.06.2020).

Atlas, S. W. (2011). The worst study ever? Exposing the scandalous methods behind an extraordinarily influential 'World Heath Report', www.commentary.org/articles/scott-atlas/the-worst-study-ever/ (accessed: 18.11.2022).

Blue Cross Blue Shield Association (2003). *The uninsured in America*. Blue Cross Blue Shield Association.

Chu, M. C., & Rhoades J. A. (2009). The uninsured in America, 1996–2008: Estimates for the US civilian noninstitutionalized population under age 65, www.meps.ahrq.gov/data_files/publications/st259/stat 259.pdf (accessed: 19.06. 2020).

Commonwealth Fund (2017). Underinsured rate increased sharply in 2016; more than two of five marketplace enrollees and a quarter of people with employer health insurance plans are now underinsured, 2016, www.commonwealthfund.org/press-release/2017/underinsured-rate-increased-sharply-2016-more-two-five-marketplace-enrollees-and (accessed: 23.06.2022).

DeNavas-Walt, C., Proctor, B. D., & Smith, J. C. (2007). *Income, poverty, and health insurance coverage in the United States: 2006.* US Census Bureau.

DeNavas-Walt, C., Proctor, B. D., & Smith, J. C. (2008). *Income, poverty, and health insurance coverage in the United States: 2007.* US Census Bureau.

DeNavas-Walt, C., Proctor, B. D., & Smith, J. C. (2013). *Income, poverty, and health insurance coverage in the United States: 2012.* US Census Bureau.

DeNavas-Walt, C., & Proctor, B. D. (2014). Income and Poverty in the United States: 2013. US Census Bureau.

Drobnic Holand, A. (2009) Number of those without health insurance about 46 million, www.politifact.com/factchecks/2009/aug/18/bar ack-obama/number-those-without-health-insurance-about-46-mil/ (accessed: 18.06.2020).

Goodman, J. C., Musgrave, G. L., & Herrick, D. M. (2004). *Lives at risk. Single-payer national health insurance around the world.* Rowman & Littlefield Publishers.

Hennessey, K. (2009). How many uninsured people need additional help from taxpayers? https://keithhennessey.com/2009/04/09/how-many-uninsured-people-need-additional-help-from-taxpayers/ (accessed: 25.06.2020).

Institute of Medicine (2003). *Hidden costs, value lost: Uninsurance in America (insuring health).* National Academies Press.

KFF (Kaiser Family Foundation) (2008). Health care costs and election 2008, www.kff.org/health-costs/issue-brief/health-care-costs-and-elect ion-2008/ (accessed: 10.06.2020).

KFF (Kaiser Family Foundation) (2019). President Trump's proclamation suspending entry for immigrants without health coverage, www. kff.org/disparities-policy/fact-sheet/president-trumps-proclamation-suspending-entry-for-immigrants-without-health-coverage/ (accessed: 24.06.2020).

Mises, L. (1998). *Human action. A treatise on economics.* Ludwig von Mises Institute.

Passel, J. S., & Cohn, D'V. (2008). Trends in unauthorized immigration: undocumented inflow now trails legal inflow, www.pewresearch.org/hispanic/2008/10/02/trends-in-unauthorized-immigration/ (accessed: 24.06.2020).

Pipes, S. C. (2008). *The top ten myths of American health care: A citizen's guide.* Pacific Research Institute.

The Pew Charitable Trusts (2016). *Household expenditures and income.* The Pew Charitable Trusts.

Pew Research Center (2009). A portrait of unauthorized immigrants in the United States, www.pewresearch.org/hispanic/2009/04/14/a-portrait-of-unauthorized-immigrants-in-the-united-states/ (accessed: 24.06.2020).

Rothbard, M. N. (2006). *Making economic sense.* Ludwig von Mises Institute.

Rytnia N./US Department of Homeland Security (2008). Estimates of the legal permanent resident population in 2007, www.dhs.gov/sites/default/files/publications/LPR%20Population%20Estimates%202007_0.pdf (accessed 24.06.2020).

SHADAC/US Census Bureau (2017). 2016 Health insurance coverage estimates, 2017, www.shadac.org/sites/default/files/publications/SHADAC%20ACS-CPS-Webinar_2017_FINALforWeb_optimized.pdf (accessed: 19.06.2020).

Smith, J. C., & Medalia, C. (2014). *Health insurance coverage in the United States: 2013.* US Census Bureau.

US Census Bureau (2019). Health insurance coverage measurement in the annual social and economic supplement to the Current Population Survey (CPS ASEC) and the American Community Survey (ACS), www.census.gov/programs-surveys/cps/technical-documentation/user-notes/health-insurance-user-notes/health-ins-cov-meas-asec-acs.html (accessed: 19.06.2020).

Whitman, G. (2010). Individual insurance mandates. In S. W. Atlas (Ed.), *Reforming America's health care system: The flawed vision of ObamaCare.* Hoover Institution Press Publication, pp. 22–30.

World Health Organization (2009). *The World Health Report 2000. Health systems: Improving performance.* World Health Organization.

2 Objectives and changes introduced by ObamaCare

Establishment of the Healthcare Insurance Marketplace

One of the key tasks of ObamaCare was to provide insurance for people who could not get insured in their workplace, for whom the cost of individual insurance was too high but who, at the same time, achieved income at a level that made it impossible to enrol in Medicaid. Due to the complexity of these conditions, a decision was made to create the so-called Healthcare Insurance Marketplaces/Exchanges to support such people in gaining access to medical services. It also influenced the perception of ObamaCare as a kind of extension of the Medicaid program. These markets/exchanges were based on several regulations mainly concerning insurance companies participating in them. However, the purpose of this section is not to reproduce all the provisions of ObamaCare, but to show them in economic terms, that is, in terms of the assumed goals and the means (regulations) used.

There are two types of marketplaces/exchanges mentioned: federal and state ones, offering the same services. It was also possible to sign up for insurance through a special platform (healthcare. gov). It also provided information on the subsidies available to insured people with lower incomes. In 2017, 11 states and the District of Columbia had their own sites, while the rest used the federal platform (Obamacare.net, 2017).

Health insurance marketplaces/exchanges are a unique creation because, despite the participation of private insurance companies, they are subject to further regulations limiting their functioning, which boils down to rigid compliance with the set rules. It is also worth emphasizing that such far-reaching interference in the activities of insurance companies did not occur in previous years on the

DOI: 10.4324/9781003385158-3

individual or group insurance market. The new regulations also apply to other areas of health care, but their scope is best reflected by the marketplaces/exchanges.

Therefore, the key regulations in this area are aimed at eliminating or limiting such actions of insurance companies that could affect some people's exclusion from insurance. While determining them, the purpose was to anticipate the possible actions of insurance companies and, on this basis, create several regulations to prevent this process. This leads to the conclusion that individual key interventions form a whole and not a random set. Their sequence and the resulting cause-and-effect relationships are well demonstrated by McGuff and Murphy (2015, p. 79):

- A mechanism to provide health insurance to (most) Americans ("universal coverage")
- Non-discriminatory pricing in health insurance premiums ("community rating")
- Minimum standards for health plans ("essential health benefits")
- A requirement that (almost) everyone obtains health insurance ("individual mandate")
- Government subsidies for the poor
- Various new taxes on "the rich" to pay for the new spending commitments
- Government guarantees for the health insurance companies
- A requirement that (some) employers provide health insurance for (some of) their employees ("employer mandate").

As it has already been mentioned, the political ambition to provide health insurance to most Americans (*universal coverage*) was focused on that part of the population that, for various reasons, did not have private insurance, but at the same time did not qualify for Medicaid – in this case, it was not about covering all Americans with uniform insurance under the government's single-payer system. Meeting this objective (1) obligated the insurance companies to accept for insurance (as part of the Healthcare Insurance Marketplace) all those willing to join it regardless of their state of health. In this case, however, there was a well-justified fear that the insurance company dealing with, for example, a person who has had a long heart disease, would expect them to pay a much higher premium than would be the case for people with a lower health risk. On the other hand, increased premiums for most people at higher risk would prove prohibitive and they would hence remain uninsured, while the regulation would be ineffective. Therefore, further regulations were introduced in the form of a significant reduction in the differentiation of premiums based on the indicated criteria (2). The so-called *community rating*, that is, the requirement to unify premiums, introduced certain limits as to their amount. Under these regulations, insurance companies could no longer differentiate premiums based on gender or health status. They were left some (limited) room for manoeuvre to change the amount of premiums based on the age of the insured, their geographical location (place of residence), or smoking status. However, even in this respect, there were certain limits. For example, the insurance company could set the premium for an elderly person at the highest level of three times the premium of a young person. In turn, the premium for a smoker could be higher by a maximum of 50% compared to the premium of a non-smoker with the same insurance (McGuff & Murphy, 2015, pp. 81–82, 85). Therefore, they were a kind of substitute for the proper risk assessment process.

However, these two regulations would not be sufficient, because insurance companies (further) trying to avoid a significant increase in expenses, could exclude some of the risks (e.g., treatment of heart disease) from the scope of insurance.

Hence, ObamaCare includes provisions on the required minimum scope of insurance (3) (*essential health benefits*). Offering insurance without the scope required by law would not be possible. All health plans offered within the Healthcare Insurance Marketplace contain ten categories of services: outpatient services; emergency services; hospitalizations (surgeries); pregnancy and maternity services; mental health services; prescription drugs; rehabilitation; laboratory services; preventive and health services including chronic diseases; and paediatric services. Furthermore, each plan can optionally include dental and ophthalmic services (HealthCare.gov, g).

Due to the large number and variety of these services, four types of plans were created: bronze, silver, gold, and platinum. Each subsequent one contains an increasingly wider range of services, a higher premium and a decreasing share of own deductibles incurred by the insured person. In the case of the bronze health insurance plan, the insurer covers 60% of the costs and the insured

40%. For the other plans, the ratio is: 70/30 (silver plan), 80/20 (gold plan) and 90/10 (platinum plan) (HealthCare.gov, f). Moreover, the so-called catastrophic plans were also created, with relatively low premiums and a large share of own costs. Their scope includes serious illnesses and the consequences of accidents, but not routine procedures. Such plans can only apply to people under the age of 30 or those who, for certain reasons, cannot purchase insurance through the Healthcare Insurance Marketplace (HealthCare.gov, a). Therefore, those individual types of plans are not the result of the activities of insurance companies, but the product of regulations which are not based on market risk assessment.

As it turns out, regulations regarding the scope of insurance lead to further problems. The requirement of minimum insurance scope along with the unification of premiums produces strong redistributive effects. Therefore, the young and the healthy subsidize older insured people with worse health, which may cause some people from the first group to resign from too expensive (for them) insurance. Therefore, it was necessary to introduce another regulation (4) in the form of an individual mandate, which had not happened in US history before. From the government's point of view, it was the only way to maintain the ability to achieve the assumed goals – otherwise many people could not join the insurance at all. However, this would not be unusual, as a similar scenario had already taken place in the past. For instance, state regulations artificially expanding insurance coverage had long been inflating premiums and, thus, discouraging the young and the healthy from joining a plan, whether in a group or individual form. Furthermore, financial penalties were introduced for not having insurance – another regulation that had not occurred earlier in US history. One of the reasons for their introduction was undoubtedly the fear that Americans, accustomed to the freedom to choose whether to have (or not) insurance, would ignore the obligation to buy it, which could lead to having too small a pool of the insured and not obtaining enough funds. In 2014 the amount of the penalty for a single person over the age of 18 was $95 or a maximum of 1% of their income. In turn, in 2016, the penalties amounted to $695 or 2.5% of income, respectively (Table 2.1).

However, there are certain exceptions to the obligation of having health insurance. Lack of insurance will not result in a financial penalty if: the insurance concluded by the employer turns out to

Table 2.1 Amounts and limits of financial penalties for lack of health insurance

Year	The amount of the penalty for lack of insurance depending on the insurance variant (USD)
2014	95 per adult, 47.50 per child (up to 18), 285 per family, or 1% of household income (the highest of these amounts will be paid)
2015	325 per adult, 162.50 per child (up to 18), 975 per family or 1% of household income (the highest of these amounts will be paid)
2016	695 per adult, 347.50 per child (up to 18), 2,085 per family or 2.5% of household income (the highest of these amounts will be paid)

Source: Own study based on: Healthcare.gov, e.

be too much an expense for the employee; the person concerned belongs to a specific religious group which makes it possible to share health costs among its members; in a situation where the uninsured person is not a legal immigrant or has the status of a prisoner. Moreover, the lack of insurance will be justified in the situation of people who: remain homeless; have declared bankruptcy; have experienced a natural disaster or their health insurance has been cancelled (Obamacare.net, 2017). The examples presented above show that covering all US residents with compulsory insurance it is not so obvious, and even a government which insists on it must consider certain exceptions in this regard.

The obligation to have extensive insurance packages would force people reluctant to this idea to buy them. However, this would be even more problematic for people with lower incomes, which would again raise fears that, contrary to the regulations, they will remain uninsured. Therefore, it was necessary to provide such people with support in the form of subsidies. This also meant additional expenditure, which required the imposition of new taxes (6) (McGuff, Murphy, 2015, p. 83) to be covered, among others, by high-premium health plans.

There are two forms of support for people with lower incomes available. The first is the Premium Tax Credit, which is granted to households with incomes between 100 and 400% of the Federal Poverty Level (FPL). The lower the income, the greater

Table 2.2 Reliefs granted to a family of four depending on their FPL (2014)

Income	Premium of the insured after the relief		
FPL (%)	FPL (USD)	Premium as % of income (maximum limit)	Monthly premium (USD)
100 – 133	23,550 – 31,322	2	39 – 52
133 – 150	31,322 – 35,325	3 – 4	78 – 118
150 – 200	35,325 – 47,100	4 – 6.3	118 – 247
200 – 250	47,100 – 58,875	6.3 – 8.1	247 – 395
250 – 300	58,875 – 70,650	8.1 – 9.5	395 – 559
300 – 350	70,650 – 82,425	9.5	559 – 652
350 – 400	82,425 – 94,200	9.5	652 – 745

Source: Own study based on: KFF, 2013.

the relief granted and the smaller the insured person's premium. For instance, a family of four with an annual income of $23,550 (100% FPL in 2014) will not pay more than 2% of their annual income for their insurance. In turn, for a family with an annual income of $ 94,200 (400% FPL), this limit amounts to 9.5% (KFF (Kaiser Family Foundation), 2013). Examples of relief amounts depending on income are provided in Table 2.2.

The insured person obtains information about the relief they are eligible for after enrolling in the selected health plan, providing their income, and so on. Technically, the relief is accrued at the time the premiums are paid and is directly redirected from the federal government to the insurer, but it is also possible to settle the relief after paying taxes (Center on Health Insurance Reforms). Most people insured as part of the Healthcare Insurance Marketplace qualify for a relief – in 2017, 84% of the insured received such support (Obamacare.net, 2017), which should not be surprising considering the target group and several introduced regulations which significantly contributed to increasing the cost of these insurances.

The second form of support for people with lower incomes is reducing their additional expenses (apart from the premium) that they incur out of their own pockets. It is possible thanks to Cost Sharing Reduction (CSR), a program which reduces expenses on deductibles, co-payment, and co-insurance. People eligible for this

Table 2.3 Reliefs a family of four is eligible for in reference to the FPL (2014)

Income	Maximum amount limit for covering expenses	Actuarial value of the plan		
FPL (%)	FPL per 1 person (USD)	Per 1 person	Per family	(%)
100 – 150	11,490 – 17,235	2,250	4,500	94
150 – 200	17,235 – 22,980	2,250	4,500	87
200 – 250	22,980 – 28,725	5,200	10,400	73

Source: Own study based on: KFF, 2014.

support are the insured with income in the range of 100–250% of FPL. However, this program only includes silver health plans.[1] As with the relief, the funds go directly from federal sources to the insurance company. The insured in lower income ranges can count on covering a much larger part of their expenses (up to a certain amount limit). For people with income corresponding to 100–150% of FPL it will be 94% of total expenses on insurance (apart from the premium). In turn, the insured with income in the range of 200–250% of FPL can count on covering 73% of such expenses (Center on Health Insurance Reforms, n. d.) (Table 2.3). Therefore, CSR significantly reduces or almost eliminates the expenses incurred by the insured out of their own pockets.

Financial support should also be extended to insurance companies because, despite clear arrangements, the regulations introduced a lot of uncertainty as to the enrolment of a sufficient number of people or costs. This, in turn, would result in lower premium income and profits. Therefore, there was a risk that without adequate government guarantees for insurance companies (7) they would not even be interested in offering insurance under the Healthcare Insurance Marketplace and, thus, might stop the whole process of change. To provide support to insurance companies, three specific (two temporary) programmes were set up: a reinsurance programme, the so-called risk corridors, and a risk adjustment programme.

The reinsurance program was aimed at maintaining the level of individual health insurance premiums at a stable level. It was related to fears of premium increases introduced by insurance companies due to the admission of all people willing to join – in accordance with the requirements of ObamaCare, that is, regardless of their health condition, and so on. This program was in force from 2014 to 2016 and consisted in the transfer of funds to more expensive individual plans. It was a kind of compensation for insurance companies who, in exchange for the funds received, were to refrain from increasing the premiums.[2] Funds for this purpose were obtained from both health insurance companies, including those dealing with the service of self-insured plans on the individual and group market. These funds went to individual insurance markets, which already operated based on new regulations, that is, the newly created Healthcare Insurance Marketplace and other individual markets. The Department of Health and Human Services (HHS) transferred them to the most expensive individual policies. A specific health plan (and insurance company) received such support when their cost exceeded a certain level – the so-called attachment point. HHS set this level at $45,000 (in 2014 and 2015) and at $90,000 in 2016.[3] Furthermore, a maximum threshold for HHS support of $2,50,000 was also introduced. The reinsurance rate was set at 80% in 2014 and at 50% in 2015 and 2016. This meant that when (in 2014) the cost of a given health plan exceeded $45,000, 80% of the additional costs above that amount were covered by the common fund, but up to the threshold of $2,50,000 – after exceeding it, all costs were still incurred by the insurance company. If the payments were lower than the sum of the funds raised, HHS increased the reinsurance rate, which finally in 2014 amounted to 100% and in 2015 to 55%. If there were surplus funds in a given year, they were transferred to the following year. On the other hand, in the event of larger claims of insurance companies exceeding the fund's resources, the reinsurance rate decreased. The total amount of funds allocated to this program decreased every year: in 2014 it was set at $10 billion, in 2015 it was $6 billion and in 2016 $4 billion (Cox et. al., 2016).

The second support programme, that is, risk corridors, was also aimed at limiting the increase in premiums and financial losses of insurance companies. and included the so-called Qualified Health Plans (QHPs), that is, health plans offered mainly as part of the Healthcare Insurance Marketplace.[4] This program worked together with the so-called Medical Loss Ratio (MLR), based on which insurance companies offering insurance for individuals or small groups were obliged to allocate at least 80% of the premium to medical care and expenses aimed at improving the quality or reimbursement of part of the premium to the insured. Funding for this program was based on insurance companies offering QHP plans (Cox et. al., 2016).

The program functioned based on the indicator being the ratio of allowable costs to the target amount based on the amount of the premium. For better clarity of the argument, it shall be referred to in the form of the abbreviation AC/TA. A ratio lower than 1 (or lower than 100%) meant that the costs were lower than the target amount (so the insurance company recorded a small profit). In turn, a result above 1 (or higher than 100%) indicated costs exceeding the target amount (in which case the insurance company incurred a loss). If the ratio of the services (costs) of a plan to its target amount based on the amount of the premium oscillated around (+/-) 3% (97–103% AC/TA), then insurance companies kept small profits or incurred insignificant losses. On the other hand, plans with even lower costs (services), that is, below the lower limit of the indicator (97%), fell into specific risk corridors. If the costs were in the range of 3–8% below the target amount of the AC/TA ratio (97–92%), the insurance company transferred 50% of its excess profits to HHS. For instance, if for a specific plan this indicator amounted to 95%, then the insurance company would be obliged to transfer half of the profits from the difference between the actual (95%) and the target (acceptable) value of the indicator (97%). On the other hand, plans with costs below 8% of the second AC/TA threshold (less than 92%) fell into the next corridor and contributed 2.5% of their target amount and 80% of the profits from the difference between the actual costs and the second lower limit of the ratio (92%) to HHS. Analogically, plans with higher costs could count on additional measures to reduce their losses in similar proportions. In the event of losses greater than the funds obtained, they were covered proportionally (Cox et. al., 2016).

The risk corridor program was a kind of start-up compensation mechanism that was to be financed exclusively by insurance companies offering QHP. In a sense, each of them was a reinsurer. Its assumptions were aimed at stopping the increase in premiums for the most expensive health plans.

In turn, the risk adjustment program aims to redistribute funds from plans that enrol people with lower health risks to plans that include people at higher risk. Based on individual risk assessments of the insured (based on age, gender, and diagnoses) an average risk assessment of the plan representing the expected expenditure is established. Subsequently, payments are made from plans with lower actuarial risk (below average) to plans with higher risk. The program is also intended to prevent risk selection, for example, in a situation where insurance companies would like to create low-risk groups outside marketplaces/exchanges, but direct groups of people with higher risk there. It covers individual insurance and insurance of small groups both within the marketplaces/exchanges and beyond. The programme has been in force since 2014 and is not temporary (Cox et. al., 2016).

The final important element of ObamaCare that deserves attention is the requirement that larger employers offer ObamaCare-compliant insurance to at least some of their employees – full-time employees in particular. This requirement, referred to as the *employer mandate* (8), applies to employers with a minimum of 50 such employees. It is also a consequence of regulations requiring everyone to be admitted to an insurance programme, which raised concerns about rising costs not only among insurance companies but also among employers. Therefore, some enterprises could resign from more expensive insurance, depriving their employees of protection. To prevent such a scenario, a decision was taken to oblige some of them to compulsorily insure their employees. Therefore, it was another regulation that had not been previously found in US history.

As it can be observed, ObamaCare regulations interfered strongly in many areas of the US health system. Folland et al. (2013, p. 398) indicate that:

> Intervention comes mainly through three activities: provision of goods and services, redistribution, and regulation. Governments have pursued each of these activities in the health economy.

The above description is entirely consistent with the assumptions of ObamaCare whose aim was to provide the uninsured with access to medical services. To achieve this, redistribution involving mainly health insurance plans and the introduction of new taxes were necessary. These, in turn, required introducing appropriate regulations significantly affecting the functioning of insurance companies and other entities.

Changes in the private health insurance market

New fiscal burdens – Cadillac Tax

Although many of the new regulations covered newly created marketplaces/exchanges (Healthcare Insurance Marketplaces), significant changes (or their announcements) also concerned individual and group (employee) insurance markets.

One such change was the plan to introduce the so-called Cadillac Tax. It was an announced 40% tax on high-cost health insurance plans to cover health plans offered by employers.[5] It was to be implemented in 2018 (KFF, 2019a, p. 16). The 40% rate was to include the *excess* of a given plan above a certain level which in 2018 was set at $10,200 for individual policies and $27,500 for family policies. Along with raising additional funds to meet the goals set by ObamaCare, its introduction was aimed at reducing the demand for extensive and expensive health plans. The hopes were that a lower demand for health insurance would allow to reduce the prices of medical services (Eastman, 2019).

However, the main assumed effect of introducing this tax was the expected increase in tax revenues from income tax and payroll tax. According to the 2018 estimates of the Congressional Budget Office, its introduction was expected to bring about $168 billion in additional revenues between 2022 and 2028 (Fronstin, 2019). The new tax was to contribute to an increase in health insurance premiums. In the light of the prospect of higher insurance costs for employers, they were to abandon more extensive scope of health plans and compensate their employees by increasing their wages. This, in turn, would increase government tax revenues and curtail their loss generated by the existing tax relief. According to estimates of the Congressional Budget Office, about 75% of the revenue generated by the new tax would come from the higher income tax and payroll tax revenues, while only the remaining 25% would come directly from the excise duty. Moreover, it was expected that the higher costs associated with the new tax (in the case of these 25% plans) would be covered by employers by reducing their employees' remuneration (Eastman, 2019). Regardless of which option employers decide on, the government will gain additional funds.

The plans to introduce a new tax were criticized for several reasons. First, they can be considered as an attempt to indirectly eliminate (partly) the tax relief. One can partly agree that this relief encourages employees to artificially expand their insurance coverage. However, this situation is primarily to blame on the pre-existing institutional conditions, which did not give Americans much choice when it came to the affordability of medical services outside of insurance.

Second, it was also pointed out that the amounts of premiums for employees' health insurance are systematically increasing, which may lead to a situation in which an increasing number of them will exceed the previously set thresholds beyond which the Cadillac tax would apply. Although these thresholds take inflation into account, it is worth remembering that health insurance premiums are growing faster than the inflation rate. Furthermore, the resistance to its introduction was because some of the existing health plans were relatively more expensive than others, such as those offered by trade unions paying high additional benefits to the insured (Eastman, 2019).

New regulations referring to large employers (employer mandate)

Requiring (almost) every American to have health insurance with certain standards could lead to a lot of confusion in the group (employee) health insurance market and cause dissatisfaction among many employees (e.g., some employers might stop offering too expensive insurance). Therefore, to avoid these negative effects, it was decided to extend the new regulations to only certain employers.

According to the new regulations, some employers were obliged to present their employees with an offer of health insurance which would be compliant with ObamaCare requirements. This obligation concerned employers employing at least 50 full-time employees (and/or their equivalent)[6] in the previous calendar year.[7]

Such employers were referred to as Applicable Large Employers (ALEs). A given employee was considered a full-time employee if in a calendar month he was on average employed for at least 30 hours a week or 130 hours a month. In the absence of an offer of insurance, a penalty of $2,000 or $3,000 for each full-time employee is imposed on the employer.[8] The employer is obliged to pay a penalty of the former type if he did not offer insurance for 95% of their full-time employees at least (and their dependents), and at least one of them received a tax relief within the Healthcare Insurance Marketplaces. In this case, the total value of the penalty was calculated based on the following formula: (the number of all full-time employees – 30 full-time employees) x $2,000. In turn, the latter type of penalty will be imposed on an employer who offered insurance to his full-time employees, but at least one of them received the already mentioned relief under the Healthcare Insurance Marketplaces. This meant a situation in which: insurance for such a person was too expensive; insurance did not have an appropriate scope, or the employee was not in the group of at least 95% of people to whom the insurance offer had been presented. In this case, the employer will pay a penalty of $3,000, but only for each uninsured full-time employee (Internal Revenue Service, b).

In other words, to avoid a financial penalty, the employer (ALE) must meet several requirements. First, they should ensure at least 95% of full-time employees and their dependents (e.g., children) the possibility of joining the insurance. Second, the insurance must cover at least 60% of health expenses (the so-called minimum value). Third, employees cannot spend more than 9.86%[9] of their income on insurance (the so-called affordable coverage) (KFF, 2019b). Otherwise, the employer will have to pay a financial penalty. For instance, a company with 500 full-time employees that does not offer them the opportunity to join health insurance will pay a penalty (in 2019) calculated based on the formula: (500 – 30) x $2,570 = $1,207,900. It is also worth emphasizing that the number of insured employees may be lower than the total number of people employed full-time and amount to, for example, 60% – then the penalty will not be charged (Cigna, 2019).

ObamaCare also created insurance options for smaller businesses – the Small Business Health Options Program (SHOP). This solution is aimed at employers employing from 1 to 50 full-time employees (or their equivalent) to help provide them with adequate insurance. Thanks to SHOP, some companies can also reduce their health insurance premiums based on the reliefs received.

To obtain such support, employers must meet several requirements, such as: offering insurance to all full-time employees; having at least one full-time employee who is not the owner, their partner, or their family member; and covering with insurance at least 70% of their employees (HealthCare.gov, d).

Changes in the individual health insurance market

The new regulations also covered the individual health insurance market operating outside the Healthcare Insurance Marketplaces. As it has already mentioned, the main purpose of marketplaces/exchanges is to provide financial support for people with lower incomes. However, with their help (through the healthcare.gov), individual insurance can also be obtained by people with higher incomes who will not be entitled to relief. Such people may also obtain insurance individually through other channels, for example: the website of a given insurance company; with the support of an insurance agent or broker, or by an online health insurance seller that allows one to compare the health plans of many insurance companies. According to the creators of the changes, the option of insuring oneself outside the marketplaces/exchanges may be more beneficial in the case of young people looking for short-term insurance; when not every plan in a given region is available for purchase on the marketplace/exchange; willingness to use the help of a local agent or broker; or in the event of a desire to purchase a catastrophic plan (ObamaCareFacts, 2014b).

It is also worth noting that health plans purchased outside the marketplaces/exchanges meet the standards set by ObamaCare. Their premiums are not determined based on gender or health status but on the age of the insured, their geographical location (place of residence) and smoking status. The required scope also remains the same. The difference boils down to the inability to receive a relief, hence people interested in buying insurance outside the marketplaces/exchanges may be the ones with higher incomes. Another common feature is the same enrolment period for a given health plan (the so-called open enrolment), which (with some exceptions) takes place in the last months of the year preceding the start of protection (ObamaCareFacts, 2014b). For instance, in 2020 enrolment periods for 2021 in most states occur between 1 November and 15 December, but they may be extended (ObamaCareFacts, 2014a).

The final issue to emphasize in this context is the so-called grandfathered health insurance plans. These are individual life insurances concluded no later than 23 March 23, 2010.[10] Formally, these plans did not meet the requirements of ObamaCare (e.g., not considering the health status of the insured when determining the premium) but, due to their popularity, the insured were allowed to continue them after 2010. However, later it was no longer possible to enrol in this type of insurance. Insurance companies could continue to have them in their offer if they did not reduce the scope of insurance or increase the costs of those previously insured. After Obamacare went into effect in 2014, these kinds of plans were not sold within Healthcare Insurance Marketplaces but through insurance companies, brokers, or agents (HealthCare.gov, c).

Changes in the pharmaceutical market

Prescription drugs (RX)

The changes introduced in the insurance market indirectly had a significant impact on the pharmaceutical market. The desire to provide insurance to previously uninsured people translated into, among other things, greater sales of prescription drugs (RX) in the future. The new regulations also covered manufacturers of original medicines, generic medicines, and other areas of their activity. Although the ObamaCare Act imposed new regulations and taxes on the American pharmaceutical industry, it ultimately gave it many benefits, which positively affected its growth prospects in the following years.

The impact of the new regulations on increasing sales of RX drugs is due to several reasons. First, ObamaCare expands eligibility for the government's Medicaid program. Second, newly created insurance marketplaces/exchanges offer most of the insured tax reliefs that significantly reduce their expenses, making insurance more affordable. This is beneficial for pharmaceutical companies because the number of the insured is increasing, and their health plans cover the purchase of this type of medication.

Third, the new regulations require insurers to have the children of the insured covered until they reach the age of 26 – before they would usually lose their insurance coverage when they turned 19. Children up to 26 remain insured even if they no longer live with their parents, they are not financially dependent on them or no longer have student status (Centers for Medicare & Medicaid Services, n. d.).

Fourth, the changes also included Medicare, Part D specifically, which is responsible for reimbursing prescription drugs to seniors. Most of these plans had a *donut hole*, which meant that after exceeding a certain limit of spending on medicines, the insured had to cover the costs of buying them out of their own pockets (HealthCare.gov, b). The mechanism was as follows: the insured senior incurred direct expenses for the purchase of prescription drugs up to $310. After exceeding this limit, 75% of the cost of medicines was covered by Medicare (Part D). The rest (25%) were paid by the insured, but up to a certain amount of $2,800. After exceeding it, seniors continued to pay 100% of the cost until the next limit of $4,550 was reached – this was the so-called *donut hole*. After exceeding this cost limit, the insured person's share fell again – this time to 5% and the remaining 95% of the costs were covered by insurance. ObamaCare introduced changes aimed at financial support for seniors who found themselves in the donut hole – first in the form of discount checks or discounts on the purchase of original medicines. By 2020, this gap was to be limited, that is, seniors were still to incur 25% (and not 100%) of the costs up to a certain limit (Medicare.gov, 2010).

Original and generic drugs

To raise new funds, ObamaCare introduced the so-called *annual fee*. It covered those pharmaceutical companies and drug importers whose total annual sales of Branded Prescription Drugs (BPDs), within specific government programs (Medicare, Medicaid, etc.), exceeded $5 million. The amount of the levy is to be determined based on the share of the producer concerned on that market, and then a reference of that share to a predetermined amount. Its amount increased over time: in 2011 it amounted to $2.5 billion, in 2014 it was $3 billion, and in 2018 $4.1 billion (Internal Revenue Service, a). For instance, a manufacturer who in 2014 held a

10% share in the sale of their drugs to the indicated government programs was obliged to pay $300 million.

The changes also covered generic drugs, specifically the process of their registration. The purpose was to limit the actions of manufacturers of original medicines who made efforts to delay the entry of competitors' products into the market. Thus, changes were made to the labelling of medicines. This was particularly important because, according to the regulations, a new generic drug had to have a label corresponding to the original drug – otherwise it could not be approved and introduced to the market. Therefore, the provisions of the legislation allowed for a registration of a generic drug if the change in the labelling of the original drug was made in a short time – that is, 60 days before the patent for the original drug expired (Santerre & Neon, 2012, p. 459).

Support for new research areas

The creators of the reform also provided funds for financing research into new drugs, therapies, and so on. To improve these processes, several institutions and initiatives were set up. One of them is the Cures Acceleration Network (CAN) led by the National Center for Advancing Translational Sciences (NCATS). The institution is designed to accelerate work on highly needed drugs and reduce barriers between searching for new solutions and conducting clinical trials. Under CAN, NCATS gives the opportunity to obtain grants for the indicated research areas in the amount of up to $15 million annually. It is also possible to award partnership awards requiring complementary funding in the proportions of 1 to 3, or flexible research awards using a special funding mechanism – other transactions (OT). OT allows for properly active management of a given project (National Center for Advancing Translational Sciences).

Within ObamaCare, financial support in the form of tax reliefs could also be obtained by companies with up to 250 employees and conducting research on new types of therapies. Their obtaining was possible as part of The Qualifying Therapeutic Discovery Project. For a given project to receive such support, it had to be positively evaluated in terms of such criteria as: the emergence of new therapies used for treatment in areas where such innovations are lacking; detection and treatment of chronic or acute diseases and conditions; limiting the long-term increase in health care costs in the USA or demonstrating significant progress in cancer treatment within 30 years. The relief granted could cover up to 50% of the expenses related to the qualified investment of a given company, and its maximum amount was $5 million. In turn, the total amount of relief was $1 billion. This kind of support was granted to qualified investments made or planned in the years 2009–2010 (Internal Revenue Service, c).

Furthermore, ObamaCare regulations prohibit insurers from denying covering the patients' cost of routine benefits that are associated with their participation in approved clinical trials for the detection and treatment of life-threatening diseases such as, for example, cancer. Nor may insurers take other measures to discriminate against such persons. These rules are to encourage a greater number of patients to participate in clinical trials. According to the creators of the changes, thanks to such regulations, pharmaceutical companies should also increase their activity in the field of research (Lewis, 2010).

Better transparency of the relationship between doctors and pharmaceutical companies

The new regulations also covered the area of cooperation between doctors and manufacturers of medicines, medical devices, and other medical devices supplied under the government's Medicare, Medicaid, and CHIP programs. A new program called the National Physician Payment Transparency Program: Open Payments[11] is piloted by the Centres for Medicare & Medicaid Services (CMS). It is part of a package of changes within ObamaCare and aims to ensure greater transparency in the health care market and to increase public awareness of the financial relationships between drug and device manufacturers and certain health care providers (including doctors). According to the authors of the changes, it is intended to limit potential conflicts of interest between doctors or hospitals and manufacturers (Centers for Medicare & Medicaid Services, 2013).

These regulations require the manufacturers to report to CMS on payments and other transfers that go to doctors or hospitals.

After receiving them, CMS makes them public on its Internet website. Moreover, manufacturers and group purchasing organizations (GPOs) are required to provide the CMS with information on doctors' shares and their investment interests in these entities. The data collection process started in August 2013 and lasted until December of the same year. The data was then sent to CMS which was supposed to make it public in September 2014 (Centers for Medicare & Medicaid Services, 2013).

The subject of the reports are one-off payments exceeding $10, or $100 in a given calendar year. Manufacturers must also indicate whether the doctors were given cash, a specific item or service, shares, a fee for a consultation service, a fee for other services, a fee for giving a paper in a conference, a fee, a gift, food, travel, educational services, a grant, and so on. In the absence of such data, these entities will be subject to a financial penalty. Doctors and other entities should receive information about themselves 45 days before its publication. They may also submit their comments or reservations (Agrawal et al., 2013, pp. 2054–2056).

Other changes

Extension of eligibility for medicaid

The final aspect worth noting is the changes in eligibility for the Medicaid program. ObamaCare focuses mainly on reducing the number of people without insurance. One of the ways to achieve this goal is the insurance marketplaces/exchanges discussed earlier. In addition to them, it was also decided to increase the coverage of the Medicaid program.

The beneficiaries of Medicaid are low-income people of all ages, including new-born babies, children and parents, pregnant women, people with disabilities, people with mental illnesses, and the poorer elderly. Eligibility for this insurance depends on the state, target group, and income earned. For instance, in 2013 working parents with incomes below 50% of FPL could be enrolled in the program in 16 states. In another 17 states, the eligibility threshold was in the range of 50–99% FPL, and in another 18 states it was equal to or higher than 100% FPL. On the other hand, people without children were usually not eligible for Medicaid (The Kaiser Commission on Medicaid and the Uninsured, 2013, pp. 6–9).

Thus, such people remained uninsured. Therefore, the new law included provisions to extend eligibility for Medicaid by creating a new group: adults under 65 whose incomes are equal to or less than 138% FPL r. Initially, ObamaCare required states to expand Medicaid, but a Supreme Court ruling issued in June 2012 lifted that obligation. Additionally, according to the judges, HHS could not withhold federal compensation funds for the traditional Medicaid program (to align it with other ObamaCare requirements) unless the state implemented a Medicaid extension (The Kaiser Commission on Medicaid and the Uninsured, 2013, p. 11).

After this ruling, states could make the decision to expand (or not) the Medicaid program. It is also worth noting that the states that decided to do so, in accordance with CMS guidelines do not have a set deadline for implementing the Medicaid extension. By 2020, 39 states, including the District of Columbia, decided to take this step. In the other 12 states Medicaid was not expanded (KFF, 2020). To relieve the financial burden on the states, the federal government pledged to cover all additional expenses associated with increasing the number of newly insured people as part of the expansion of Medicaid. The federal government's involvement in covering these expenses was to gradually decrease and reach 90% in 2020 (Lyon et al., 2014, p. 662).

Furthermore, regardless of the decision to expand Medicaid, as of 2014, all states had to adopt and implement several provisions required by ObamaCare. They were aimed at better adapting the Medicaid program to the new requirements. For instance, states had to stop using their own methods of calculating income, and switch to Modified Adjusted Gross Income (MAGI) instead, which was consistent with the definition of the tax code. Another change introduced was the obligation to use a single, simplified application for Medicaid, CHIP, or other insurance available on marketplaces/exchanges developed by the HHS secretary – unless some states were allowed to use their own applications. Applicants for such insurance should also be allowed to apply online, by telephone, fax, post, or in person. They also needed to improve the registration process by eliminating face-to-face interviews and property tests and, in the first place, rely on the use of electronic data rather than physical documents to verify the eligibility criteria. These adjustments required further expenses, 90% of which were covered by the federal government (The Kaiser Commission on Medicaid and the Uninsured, 2013, p. 12).

Notes

1 At the same time, these are popular health plans.
2 In some way it can also be considered other subsidies for the insured.
3 This amount was increased due to lower premiums in two former years.
4 Health plans offered outside the Healthcare Insurance Marketplace could also qualify for the QHP if they met certain criteria.
5 It was also to cover funds going to medical (health) savings accounts.
6 The so-called Full-Time Equivalents (FTEs). It is worth noting that the regulations consider different methods of calculating FTE status. Since these calculations can be complicated, legal assistance in this aspect is often recommended.
7 This law came into force in 2016. In 2014 and 2015, employers employing 50 to 99 full-time employees were not obliged to offer them insurance of certain standards, and those employing more than 100 such employees were obliged to do so if they offered insurance for at least 70% of them.
8 The amounts of penalties are indexed each year.
9 As of 2019.
10 The date President Obama signed the Patient Protection and Affordable Care Act, or ObamaCare.
11 Also known as the so-called Sunshine Act.

References

Agrawal S., N., & Budetti, P. (2013). 'The Sunshine Act – effects on physicians', *New England Journal of Medicine, 368*: 2054–2057.
Center on Health Insurance Reforms (n .d.) How premium tax credits and cost-sharing reductions work, https://navigatorguide.georgetown. edu/how-do-premium-tax-credits-and-cost-sharing-reductions-work (accessed: 17.07.2020).
Centers for Medicare & Medicaid Services (n. d.). Young adults and the Affordable Care Act: Protecting young adults and eliminating burdens on families and businesses, www.cms.gov/CCIIO/Resources/Files/adu lt_child_fact_sheet (accessed: 27.07.2020).
Centers for Medicare & Medicaid Services (2013). Affordable Care Act 'Sunshine' rule increases transparency in health care, www.cms.gov/ newsroom/press-releases/affordable-care-act-sunshine-rule-increases-transparency-health-care (accessed: 29.07.2020).

Cox, C. et al. (2016). Explaining health care reform: Risk adjustment, reinsurance, and risk corridors, www.kff.org/health-reform/issue-brief/explaining-health-care-reform-risk-adjustment-reinsurance-and-risk-corridors/ (accessed: 20.07.2020).

Cigna (2019) Employer mandate. Fact Sheet, www.cigna.com/assets/docs/about-cigna/informed-on-reform/employer-mandate-fact-sheet.pdf (accessed: 23.07.2020).

Eastman, S. (2019) The 'Cadillac' tax and the income tax exclusion for employer-sponsored insurance, https://taxfoundation.org/cadillac-tax-employer-sponsored-health-insurance/ (accessed: 22.07.2020).

Folland, S., Goodman, A. C., & Stano, M. (2013). *The economics of health and health care* (7th ed.). Pearson.

Fronstin, P. (2019). Will the Cadillac tax generate revenue? www.ebri.org/content/will-the-cadillac-tax-generate-revenue (accessed: 23.07.2020).

HealthCare.gov (n. d. a) Catastrophic health plans, www.healthcare.gov/choose-a-plan/catastrophic-health-plans/ (accessed: 16.07.2020).

HealthCare.gov (n. d. b) Donut Hole, Medicare prescription drug, www.healthcare.gov/glossary/donut-hole-medicare-prescription-drug/ (accessed: 28.07.2020).

HealthCare.gov (n. d. c). Grandfathered health insurance plans, www.healthcare.gov/health-care-law-protections/grandfathered-plans/ (accessed: 24.07.2020).

HealthCare.gov (n. d. d). Small Business Health Options Program (SHOP), www.healthcare.gov/glossary/shop-small-business-health-options-program/ (accessed: 23.07.2020).

Healthcare.gov (n. d. e). The fee for not having health insurance, www.healthcare.gov/fees/fee-for-not-being-covered/ (accessed: 20.07.2020).

HealthCare.gov (n. d. f). The 'metal' categories: Bronze, Silver, Gold & Platinum, www.healthcare.gov/choose-a-plan/plans-categories/ (accessed: 16.07.2020).

HealthCare.gov (n. d. g). What Marketplace health insurance plans cover, www.healthcare.gov/coverage/what-marketplace-plans-cover/ (accessed: 16.07.2020).

Internal Revenue Service (n. d. a). Annual fee on branded prescription drug manufacturers and importers, www.irs.gov/affordable-care-act/annual-fee-on-branded-prescription-drug-manufacturers-and-importers (accessed: 28.07.2020).

Internal Revenue Service (n. d. b). Employer shared responsibility provisions, www.irs.gov/affordable-care-act/employers/employer-shared-responsibility-provisions (accessed: 23.07.2020).

Internal Revenue Service (n. d. c). Qualifying therapeutic discovery projects basic information: Questions and answers, www.irs.gov/newsroom/qualifying-therapeutic-discovery-projects-basic-information-questions-and-answers (accessed: 28.07.2020).

The Kaiser Commission on Medicaid and the Uninsured (2013). *Medicaid: A primer. Key information on the nation's health coverage program for low-income people.* Kaiser Family Foundation.

KFF (Kaiser Family Foundation) (2013). Premium tax credits: Answers to frequently asked questions, www.kff.org/wp-content/uploads/sites/2/2013/10/qa-on-premium-credits.pdf (accessed: 17.07.2020).

KFF (Kaiser Family Foundation) (2014). Key facts you need to know about: Cost-sharing reductions, www.healthreformbeyondthebasics.org/wp-content/uploads/2014/09/KeyFacts-Cost-Sharing-Reductions_updated2014.pdf (accessed: 17.07.2020).

KFF (Kaiser Family Foundation) (2019a) *Employer Health Benefits 2019 Annual Survey.* Kaiser Family Foundation.

KFF (Kaiser Family Foundation) (2019b) Employer responsibility under the Affordable Care Act, www.kff.org/infographic/employer-responsibility-under-the-affordable-care-act/ (accessed: 23.07.2020).

KFF (Kaiser Family Foundation) (2020). Status of state action on the Medicaid expansion decision, www.kff.org/health-reform/state-indicator/state-activity-around-expanding-medicaid-under-the-affordable-care-act/?currentTimeframe=0&sortModel=%7B%22colId%22:%22Location%22,%22sort%22:%22asc%22%7D (accessed: 29.07.2020).

Lewis, M. (2010). Healthcare reform law: Impact on pharmaceutical manufacturers, www.morganlewis.com/-/media/files/publication/law flashclient-alert/washington-government-relations-and-public-policy-lawflash/washgrpp_impactonpharmamanufacturers_lf_15apr10.pdf (accessed: 28.07.2020).

Lyon, S. M., Douglas, I. S., & Cooke, C. R. (2014). 'Medicaid expansion under the Affordable Care Act. Implications for insurance-related disparities in pulmonary, critical care, and sleep', *Annals of the American Thoracic Society, 4*: 661–667.

McGuff, D., & Murphy, R. P. (2015). *The primal prescription: Surviving the 'sick care' sinkhole.* Primal Blueprint Publishing.

Medicare.gov (2010). What is the Donut Hole?, www.medicare.gov/blog/what-is-the-donut-hole (accessed: 28.07.2020).

National Center for Advancing Translational Sciences (n. d.). Cures Acceleration Network, https://ncats.nih.gov/funding/review/can (accessed: 28.07.2020).

ObamaCareFacts.com (2014a). ObamaCare open enrollment period, https://obamacarefacts.com/obamacare-open-enrollment/ (accessed: 24.07.2020).

ObamaCareFacts.com (2014b). Private health plans outside the Marketplace, https://obamacarefacts.com/private-health-plans-outs ide-the-marketplace/ (accessed: 24.07.2020).

Obamacare.net (2017). Obamacare explained, https://obamacare.net/ obamacare-explained/ (accessed: 16.07.2020).

Santerre, R. E., & Neun, S. P. (2012). *Health economics: Theory, insights, and industry studies.* Cengage Learning.

3 Effects of the changes introduced by ObamaCare

Quasi-market Healthcare Insurance Marketplace

Death spiral (accessibility spiral) – a classic course of the process

One of the most frequently discussed effects of ObamaCare is creating a phenomenon called a death spiral in newly created exchanges/markets. However, to better understand the course of this process, it is necessary to briefly present the essence of this phenomenon and the factors that may contribute to its induction.

In its classic version, death spiral is a phenomenon characteristic of the health insurance market. It consists in the fact that the group of insured people with the same or similar health risk (standard risk) is joined by other people with a higher risk (substandard risk) at the same premium level. Therefore, the relationship between the represented risk and the appropriate amount of the premium is disturbed. The people with substandard risk, due to a worse state of health (e.g., previously occurring diseases, etc.) should be charged a higher premium or even not be insured at all because, in their case, there is a higher probability (or even certainty) of the occurrence of an insured event in the form of an illness or an accident. This, in turn, results in an increased demand for medical services for such people and, thus, higher expenses on the side of the insurers. Consequently, insurers then increase premiums to remain profitable or avoid suffering losses. What is significant, these increases cover both people with standard and substandard risk. However, for some insured people from the first group (often young and healthy), premiums become too high in relation to their relatively low health risk. Therefore, they resign from a given insurance or switch to its lower scope with a lower

DOI: 10.4324/9781003385158-4

premium. This, in turn, causes that the insurer's revenues from which it covers growing expenses decrease. Therefore, another disproportion between revenues and expenses arises and, to compensate for it, the insurer (again) increases premiums. Such actions, however, lead to further resignation from insurance, which somehow forces further increases in premiums, and so on. Hence, it is a vicious circle called the death spiral. At its final stage, only the most determined people remain insured – if the insurer does not close the entire program earlier. In this case, the spiral has a dynamic course during which insurance becomes less and less affordable for at least some of the people covered by a given health plan – which gives rise to another name for this process, that is, the spiral of affordability.[1]

The main reason for the occurrence of this phenomenon is negative selection, that is, the admission to insurance of people with higher or unacceptable health risks, which should be considered a mistake on the part of the insurance company. To reduce the negative selection, the insurer should, therefore, improve the risk assessment process. It should also be emphasized that insurers can react quickly to this type of situation, which is why the occurrence of a death spiral is not frequent and may concern selected insurance products.

It is also possible that the death spiral covers the entire system or group of insurers, for example, because of economic crises which have a negative impact on the income of young and relatively healthy people for whom having health insurance does not have to be high in the hierarchy of their needs (McKeown, 2013, p. 83).

Yet another reason for the death spiral to occur because of the negative selection may be government regulations covering the health insurance market (e.g., obligation to admit ill people for insurance, etc.). Then the increase in premiums and the loss of some of the insured is not the result of an incorrect risk assessment process, but a consequence of the requirements set by regulators.

It is also worth emphasizing that the death spiral can have a dynamic course (e.g., several years) or even last several decades. The latter case may occur, for example, in a situation where the insurer offering insurance in the individual variant prevents subsequent clients from joining such a plan (the so-called *closed block*). As a result, new (young and healthy) people can no longer join the pool of the insured. In the course of time and the withdrawal of more insured persons from insurance, more and more people with higher health risks remain, which leads to an increase in premiums. The insurer may also prolong this process by covering losses from other sources (French & Smith, 2015, pp. 60–72).

ObamaCare regulations and the death spiral

Because the death spiral can be considered a consequence of the earlier appearance of negative selection, the creators of the reform faced a considerable challenge to avoid this negative phenomenon. In this context, the key ObamaCare regulations described in the previous subsection should be considered as elements to prevent an increase in premiums in many fields. The negative selection could not be withdrawn, as this would be contrary to the paramount objective of the legislation, namely, covering previously uninsured and chronically ill people with insurance. Hence, it should come as no surprise that government secured finances which were to be a kind of compensation for insurers who, in return, were not to increase premiums and subsidies for people with lower incomes. Also, the obligation to have insurance was to increase the number of insured people with lower health risk subsidizing those with a higher risk. In turn, the same insurance coverage was to prevent potential migrations from one health plan to another.

The creators of the reform were aware of all these negative consequences, hence such a wide range of changes introduced. From an economic perspective, however, it should be emphasized that these changes could have led not so much to the cessation of the death spiral (and the laws of economics being put into motion), but only to an attempt to shift the economic burden of its impact to other social groups than those insured within the exchanges/markets. In this sense, as it will be demonstrated later in this section, the death spiral induced by ObamaCare did not occur in its classic form. However, this should not come as a surprise due to its non-market causes. It should also be emphasized that what was responsible for the non-classical development of this phenomenon were many factors occurring with a delay as well as the decisions taken, among others, by insurers or households in conditions of high uncertainty.

Interestingly, the insurance market had been struggling with the problem of negative selection caused by government regulations for a long time. In many states, the number of laws requiring ever-expanding coverage of benefits had been steadily increasing. In addition, long before ObamaCare, in 1990–1996, 16 states passed legislation significantly facilitating the possibility of joining insurance for people with health problems. This has led to a situation in which the increase in the number of uninsured was eight times higher in these states compared to states that had not introduced similar regulations. This was mainly because some healthy people stopped insuring themselves – thanks to more *liberal* regulations requiring insurers to cover with insurance also people who were already ill. Therefore, healthy people did not feel so much pressure associated with buying insurance. Then, because of the decrease in the pool of healthy insured people, premiums began to rise, causing further departures and further increases in premiums (Goodman et al., 2004, p. 218). Insurance was becoming less and less attractive to people with low health risks, which is one of the effects of the death spiral. This phenomenon was, therefore, caused by the growing negative selection in many states and was related to the whole system, that is, it did not concern a single insurer or health plan.

The increase in the number (and percentage) of the uninsured continued to progress, which caused increasing concern and political pressure. At the same time, the number of people with private insurance was constantly decreasing. Between 2000 and 2010 it fell from 205.5 million to 196 million insured with an ever-growing population. David A. Hyman and Charles Silver also point out that the smaller number of the insured had some (positive) impact on the decline in the growth rate of health care spending. At the beginning of the twenty-first century (2002) it was about 10%, while later it was systematically falling to reach about 3% in 2013 (Hyman & Silver, 2018, p. 289).

Undoubtedly, these events did not escape the attention of politicians and were one of the reasons for the desire to introduce further regulations. What was ignored, however, was the fact that it was the state regulations that largely contributed to triggering negative selection and the beginning of a cycle of the death spiral. The problem with ObamaCare was that the same measures were used to combat old problems, but on a larger scale.

Death spiral stage I – increase in the premiums

The analysis of the death spiral in the marketplaces/exchanges can be broken down into several stages occurring right after each other or in parallel. This will allow for a better understanding of the complexity of this phenomenon.

Although the negative selection was a fact, insurers did not immediately go to a significant increase in premiums. This was, among other things, because they needed time to adapt to new conditions, obtain the right amount of data on the number of the insured and costs, or test government support programs to choose a specific pricing strategy.

However, as it turned out, the increases were only a matter of time for several reasons. One of them was that insurers had limited possibilities to differentiate premiums based on individual criteria. For instance, the premium charged to older insured people could be up to three times higher than that of younger insured people. Meanwhile, before ObamaCare, the market standard was not 3 to 1, but 5 to 1. One 2013 study estimated that this restriction could result in an annual premium increase for those aged 21–27 by $850. In turn, for those aged 57–64, the premium could drop by $1,770 (McGuff & Murphy, 2015, pp. 92–93).

Other estimates, published by the Manhattan Institute in 2013, also pointed to an increase in premiums for younger insured people between 2014 and 2013 due to ObamaCare's entry into effect. These estimates compare the cheapest plans of 2013[2] for women and men aged 27, 40, and 64 to the estimated premiums in 2014 (Manhattan Institute). Although they did not fully reflect the entire scope of changes, they clearly indicated a significant (i.e., at least a double-digit) increase for younger people in most states. For instance, the state with the highest projected growth was Nevada, where for a 27-year-old man the projected premium increase was estimated at 289% (from $71 to $276) and for a 40-year-old man, 183% (from $119 to $337). In turn, the estimated premiums for 27- and 40-year-old women increased by 106% (from $134 to $276) and 194% (from $174 to $337), respectively. Data published by researchers at the Manhattan Institute clearly show that ObamaCare laid the groundwork for future partial abandonments of health insurance plans for young and healthy individuals. Interestingly, the increases in premiums were also to affect many people aged 64. On the other

Table 3.1 Selected projected increases in individual health insurance premiums (USD) before and after ObamaCare (2013–2014)

State	Age	Gender	Premium (USD) before ACA – 2013	Premium (USD) in the first year of ACA – 2014	Change
Arkansas	27	M	54.96	192.41	250.1%
	27	F	91.64	192.41	110%
	40	M	81.90	234.64	186.5%
	40	F	125.81	234.64	86.5%
	64	M	287.94	550.80	91.3%
	64	F	268.20	550.80	105.4%
Indiana	27	M	165.82	210.97	27.2%
	27	F	210.69	210.97	0.1%
	40	M	223.60	257.27	15.1%
	40	F	333.69	257.27	-22.9%
	64	M	712.21	603.92	-15.2%
	64	F	692.51	603.92	-12.8%
Nevada	27	M	71.71	276.85	286.1%
	27	F	134.96	276.85	105.1%
	40	M	119.91	337.60	181.6%
	40	F	174.90	337.60	93%
	64	M	353.10	792.50	124.4%
	64	F	345.17	792.50	129.6%
Utah	27	M	109.62	175.79	60.4%
	27	F	112.93	175.79	55.7%
	40	M	161.27	187.04	16%
	40	F	161.27	187.04	16%
	64	M	362.38	379.40	4.7%
	64	F	362.38	379.40	4.7%

Source: Own study, based on: Manhattan Institute, a.

hand, the estimated reductions in premiums covered only a few states (Table 3.1).

Another reason for such significant increases in premiums was that insurance coverage within exchanges/markets covered people with high health risks, while some of them (before 2014) had been refused admission to insurance due to serious and pre-existing health problems (Hyman & Silver, 2018, p. 292). For instance, according to a study published in mid-2014 in the *Wall Street Journal*, the percentage of people with serious illnesses amounted to 27% for the insured on marketplaces/exchanges and 21% for the insured with ObamaCare-compliant plans outside of them. Meanwhile, in the case of individual *grandfathered plans*, the percentage of such people was 12% and 16% for renewed (previously cancelled) plans (Mathews & Weaver, 2014). This is important because a relatively small percentage of insured people generates a larger part of expenses. It is worth noting that in the USA only 10% of the population consumes about 72% of health expenses, and those most in need of medical services, constituting 2% of the population, use as much as 41% of health expenses (Goodman et al., 2004, pp. 276–277).

This leads to the clear conclusion that even a small number of insured people with a high health risk can trigger a significant increase in premium prices. Therefore, such a noticeable increase in the premiums a few years after the creation of exchanges/markets should not come as a surprise. For instance, in the years 2014–2020 the average amount of the premium for the most popular silver plan for a 40-year-old man increased from $273 to $462 (up 69%). The growth itself was not linear, it reached its peak (so far) in 2018, when the average premium increased to $481 (up 76%). There were also states where these increases were much higher (e.g., Iowa – 193%) and more moderate (New Jersey – 21%) (Table 3.2).

The increase in premiums is even more noticeable for younger insured people, for example, the premium for a 27-year-old man (silver plan) increased by an average of 78% over the same period (Figure 3.1). For comparison, the CPI for medical care increased by less than 19% (FRED, b) and the CPI itself by 10% over the same period (FRED, a). Moreover, these increases would be even higher taking 2013 as the base year rather than 2014.

Premiums for insurance in family variants also increased significantly. For instance, the average insurance premium for a family of 4 increased from $810 in 2015 (Avery et al., 2015) to $1,520 in 2020 (up 88%) (Centers for Medicare & Medicaid Services, 2019b).

The problem of negative selection was exacerbated even more by a much lower than expected number of subscriptions to individual plans. In 2015, it did not yet lead to significant increases in premiums, as insurers did not have sufficient data (e.g., on burden of losses). However, as Robert Laszewski – an insurance expert and president of Health Policy and Strategy Associates – points out, already in 2015 worrying information began to appear, heralding significant increases in premiums. The first signal was, as

Table 3.2 Average increase in premiums on marketplaces/exchanges in 2014–2020 (USD)

Year	2014	2015	2016	2017	2018	2019	2020	Change
Average premium	273	276	299	359	481	478	462	69%
States with the highest premium increases								
Iowa	253	265	300	379	713	762	742	193%
Nebraska	249	296	332	507	767	838	711	185%
Oklahoma	213	226	306	518	659	696	601	182%
Tennessee	197	233	287	472	743	548	511	159%
Hawaii	183	262	262	330	438	493	474	159%
States with the lowest premium Increases								
Rhode Island	293	263	263	261	311	336	332	13%
Indiana	328	323	282	278	339	339	387	18%
New Jersey	323	316	332	348	413	352	392	21%
Arkansas	294	285	298	281	364	378	365	24%
Massachusetts	268	261	257	250	316	332	343	28%

Source: Own study, based on: Kaiser Family Foundation/KFF, a.

Note: The data refers to the second lowest variant of the 2nd Lowest Cost Silver plan for a 40-year-old non-smoking man with an annual income of $30,000 (data from HealthCare.gov and data shared by individual states) – benchmark.

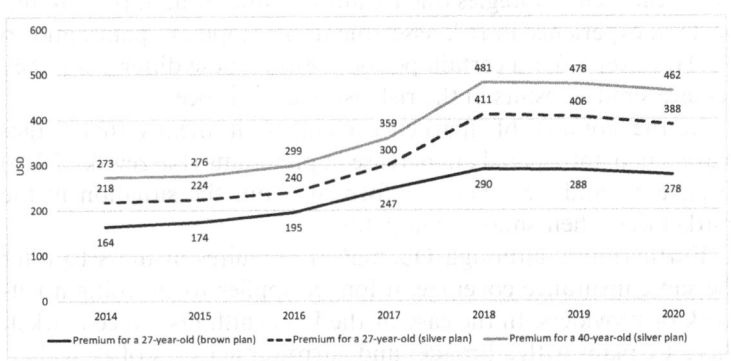

Figure 3.1 Comparison of premium increases for selected plans in 2014–2020

Note: The data refers to the second lowest variant of the 2nd Lowest Cost Silver plan for a 40-year-old non-smoking man with an annual income of $30,000 (data from HealthCare.gov and data shared by individual states) – benchmark; 2nd Lowest Cost Silver and Lowest Cost Plan for a 27-year-old non-smoker man with annual income in the amount of $25,000 (data from HealthCare.gov); The given amounts of contributions do not take into account the tax reliefs granted.

Source: Own study, based on: Kaiser Family Foundation, a.

already mentioned, lower registration for new plans. On the insurance market, the norm is to cover at least 75% of people eligible for insurance. Meanwhile in markets/exchanges, this indicator was achieved only in Vermont (75%), while in the other states it was clearly lower. In Iowa, for example, it was only 20%. It is important because enrolment slowed significantly in 2015 (10–20%) in most states, which was significantly different from ObamaCare's goals of having the number of insureds twice as high (Laszewski, 2015).

Furthermore, Laszewski emphasizes that the highest increases in premiums (15–35%) were signalled by insurers with the largest shares in markets/exchanges, where the number of people entitled to this type of insurance significantly differs from 75% (Table 8). Although in 2016 the average increase in premiums (Table 3.3) amounted to 8%, the higher increases reported by these entities should not be underestimated because they have the largest amount of data that most fully reflects the risk structure and costs. Another issue is that insurers are operating in conditions of uncertainty, which means that the plans for these increases did not result from a price collusion – therefore, smaller players did not expect such actions from their competitors. Insurers can choose significantly different strategies due to, among other things, the amount of data, experience in risk assessment, development plans, and so on. However, after a certain period, despite these differences, they achieve similar results in the risk assessment process.

In the context of markets/exchanges, it means that larger players had anticipated an increase in premiums (Laszewski, 2015) in advance and were better informed about the situation in the market than their smaller competitors.

Furthermore, although ObamaCare requires insurers to offer the same insurance coverage, it longer applies to choosing a network of providers. In the case of the US health insurance market, there are plans with a broader and narrower network of providers. More limited networks enable insurers to reduce costs and are present in plans such as Health Maintenance Organizations (HMOs) and Exclusive Provider Organizations (EPO). In turn, plans with a wider choice of suppliers include Preferred Provider Organizations (PPO) and Point of Service (POS) – they are relatively more expensive than HMO or EPO, but they give the opportunity to use medical services also outside a given network. Therefore, for the insured, the choice of insurance with a limited network of

Table 3.3 Reported/estimated premium increases by major insurers by state for 2016

Insurer	State	Description	Percentage of state-insured persons of all eligible persons
CareFirst Blue Cross of Maryland	Maryland	The insurer reported a 34% increase for its PPO plan and a 26.7% increase for its HMO plan. CareFirst has an 80% share of the state's market/exchange.	30%
Moda; Lifewise	Oregon	The largest insurer with a 52% market/exchange share, Moda, reported a 25.6% premium increase. Lifewise, with a 19% market share, reported a 38.5% increase.	35%<
Blue Cross Blue Shield of Tennessee; Humana	Tennessee	Blue Cross Blue Shield of Tennessee with a 70% market share plans to increase premiums by an average of 36.3%. In turn, the second largest insurer, Humana, reports a 15.8% increase.	40%<
Humana	Georgia	Humana, which has a 53% share in the state market, reports increases in the range of 14.8-19.4%	n.d.
Wellmark Blue Cross; Coventry	Iowa	Wellmark Blue Cross is asking for approval for increases of around 43% and Coventry by 18%.	25%
Insurance Department	Kansas	The Kansas Insurance Department said premiums would increase by about 38%.	40%<
Highmark; Geisinger HMO	Pennsylvania	The state's market leader, Highmark, reported increases from 13.5% to 39.65%. Another insurer, Geisinger HMO, planned to increase premiums from 40.6% to 58.4%.	50%

(Continued)

Table 3.3 (Continued)

Insurer	State	Description	Percentage of state-insured persons of all eligible persons
Primera Blue Cross; Coordinated Care; Lifewise; Regence	Washington	The market leader, Primera Blue Cross, reports premiums higher by 9.6%. Other major insurers in the state (Coordinated Care, Lifewise, Regence) are withdrawing their plans and replacing them with new ones. The scope of premium changes for other plans ranges from 10.86% to 19.3%.	30%
Anthem; Connecticare	Connecticut	Anthem, with a 33% market share, reported a 6.7% increase, with the second largest player, Connecticare, up 2%. Other increases range from 5.2% to 33%.	45%
Blue Cross Blue Shield (BCBS)	Michigan	The market leader, BCBS with a 65% market share, reports increase for its two plans of 9.7% and 11.3%. Other changes in premiums range from -12.6% to 42.2%.	45%
Blue Cross Blue Shield (BCBS)	Vermont	BCBS reports increases of 8.3%. Other changes in premiums range from 4.7% to 14.3%.	75%

Source: Own study, based on: Laszewski, 2015.

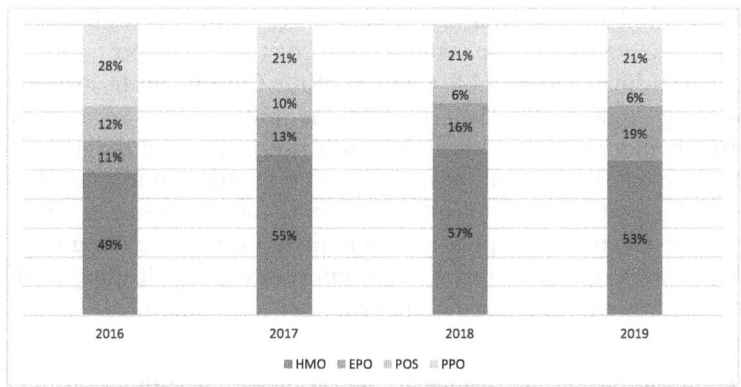

Figure 3.2 Participation of individual health plans under Healthcare Insurance Marketplace

Source: Own study based on: Carpenter, Sloan, 2018.

suppliers may prove problematic if they want to use the services of a specific doctor, and so on. In the context of ObamaCare, this is particularly important because, according to research published by the analytical company Avalere, most health plans on the marketplaces/exchanges are HMO and EPO plans, that is, with a narrower network of suppliers. Moreover, the participation of HMOs as well as EPO has increased in recent years while PPO and POS have decreased (Figure 3.2) (Carpenter & Sloan, 2018).

The situation is different for plans concluded by the employer, where the share of PPO and POS is much higher and in 2019 it amounted to 52% and 9% respectively, while the share of HMO is only 12% (KFF, 2019c). Thus, a larger share of plans with a wider network of suppliers in marketplaces/exchanges would undoubtedly be reflected in higher premiums.

Furthermore, insurers began to use different practices to discourage people with poor health from choosing their health plans. One study demonstrated that an easy way to identify such insured people is through their reported demand for prescription drugs. Then, insurers created, for example, non-transparent electronic forms for such people, which made it difficult for them to enrol in given health plans. Moreover, such health plans did not cover the purchase of drugs needed by the chronically ill; had a larger number of mandatory substitutes or higher shares in direct expenses incurred by the insured (Geruso et al., 2019, pp. 64–107).

According to Michael F. Cannon of the Cato Institute, insurers offering high-quality health plans is problematic because it attracts more people with high health risk generating the highest costs, that is, patients suffering from, among others: multiple sclerosis, rheumatoid arthritis, infertility, and other expensive diseases. As a result, insurers apply higher limits on direct spending (e.g., deductible), narrow networks of suppliers excluding leading medical centres, or imprecise supplier catalogues (Cannon, 2017).

Death spiral stage II – higher tax reliefs for people with lower incomes

A significant increase in premiums also translated into higher tax credits (Advanced Premium Tax Credit – APTC) received by the insured with income in the range of 100–400 FPL. Without this support, they would not have been able to cover higher premiums (both in the first year of ObamaCare and subsequent years), which would result in their resignation from insurance. In other words, the amount of tax credit had to increase so that the part of the premium paid by the insured remained at the same level or

Table 3.4 Average amount of tax credit granted (APTC) in 2015–2020

Year	Average monthly premium for insured persons eligible for APTC	Average amount of APTC	Premium after considering APTC	Ratio of APTC to the premium	The number of people eligible for APTC
2015	$374	$268	$105	72%	6,502,118
2016	$408	$294	$113	72%	7,071,600
2017	$489	$383	$106	78%	7,190,000
2018	$639	$550	$89	86%	7,447,615
2019	$626	$539	$87	86%	7,325,211
2020	$606	$517	$89	85%	7,205,225

Source: Own study, based on: Kaiser Family Foundation, b; Annual data published by the Department of Health and Human Services on the number of insured persons under the Healthcare Insurance Marketplaces.

Note: The table contains data on premiums for insured persons entitled to APTC in states that used the site HealthCare.gov in individual years.

only slightly changed. The largest increase in the amount of tax credit granted took place in 2017–2018, that is, during a period of a significant increase in premiums. In turn, the decrease in the amount of tax credit granted in 2019–2020 was accompanied by a slight decrease in the amount of premiums on the marketplaces/ exchanges (Table 3.4).

In six years, the APTC increased by 93%, while the premium increased by 62%. There is also a noticeable tendency towards a decreasing premium of the insured. This should not be surprising as, for example, out of all 8.2 million insured by HealthCare. gov in 2020, as many as 71% achieved income equivalent to 100–250% FPL (Centers for Medicare & Medicaid Services, 2020). Therefore, it required the involvement of more and more government funds because insurers set higher and higher premiums regardless of the distribution of expenses between the insured and the government.

Significant increases in the amount of tax credits were already visible in 2017. This was related to, for example, the expiry (in 2016) of two government support programs for insurers: risk corridors and the reinsurance program. Therefore, insurers had to increase premiums to compensate for the lost revenue sources. In most states, increases (in percentage terms) were double-digit and in 11 even triple-digit. Only four states recorded declines (Table 3.5) (Kamal et al., 2017).

Therefore, additional expenses related to the increase in insurance premiums do not include the insured who are entitled to APTC – the difference is covered by the government and by taxpayers. Otherwise, many insured through marketplaces/ exchanges would quickly abandon their health plans. This is also one of the reasons why the death spiral on the markets/exchanges differs from the classic one – all additional expenses are there covered by the insured themselves.

In addition, there were difficulties related to the settlement of granted tax credits, which influenced the increase in government spending. Initially, the amount of tax credit granted is determined at the time of enrolment in a given health plan for the next year, that is, between November and December of the old (base) year. Subsequently, households that have received such support must submit additional forms when settling accounts with the tax office in April of the following year, which is to confirm that they receive

Table 3.5 Five largest increases/decreases in the amount of tax credits in 2017 and their impact on the premiums paid by the insured

5 largest increases in APTC height (%)

State	Premium before the (APTC) 2016	Premium after the tax credit 2017	Change	Tax credit (APTC) 2016	2017	Change	Costs of the insured 2016	2017	Change
Minnesota	235 $	366 $	55%	208 $	207 $	0%	27 $	159 $	481%
Kansas	248 $	361 $	46%	208 $	207 $	0%	40 $	154 $	287%
Alabama	288 $	492 $	71%	208 $	207 $	0%	80 $	285 $	256%
Oklahoma	295 $	493 $	67%	208 $	207 $	0%	87 $	286 $	230%
Pennsylvania	276 $	418 $	51%	208 $	207 $	0%	68 $	211 $	209%
5 Largest decreases/smallest increases in APTC height (%)									
Ohio	234 $	229 $	-2%	208 $	207 $	0%	26 $	22 $	-17%
Indiana	298 $	286 $	-4%	208 $	207 $	0%	90 $	79 $	-12%
Massachusetts	250 $	247 $	-1%	208 $	207 $	0%	42 $	40 $	-5%
Rhode Island	263 $	261 $	-1%	208 $	207 $	0%	55 $	54 $	-2%
Arkansas	310 $	314 $	1%	208 $	207 $	0%	102 $	107 $	4%
States in which APTC appeared									
Arizona	207 $	507 $	145%	207 $	207 $	0%	0 $	300 $	-
Illinois	198 $	291 $	48%	198 $	207 $	5%	0 $	84 $	-
New Mexico	186 $	258 $	39%	186 $	207 $	11%	0 $	51 $	-

Source: Own study, based on: Cox et al., 2016a.

Note: The data is for the second lowest variant of the 2nd Lowest Cost Silver plan for a 40-year-old non-smoking man with an annual income of $30,000.

income that falls within a certain range of FPL, entitling them to a greater or lesser tax credit (Internal Revenue Service, c).

However, as Brian Blase of the Mercatus Center at George Mason University points out, in 2015 (for 2014 tax returns), only 8% of the people eligible for APTC received the correct amount of tax credit. Just over half of them reported understated income and had to make an appropriate return to the IRS of an average of $860, while the remaining 41% of people declared too high income and received from the IRS a return of an average of $640. In addition, by the end of October 2015, about 1.4 million households had not correctly determined their 2014 relief – 2/3 of them filed a tax return with the IRS, but without an additional form, and the remaining 1/3 did not submit any documents (Blase, 2016).

The situation was similar when filing tax returns in April 2016. According to estimates, the total amount of APTC granted amounted to $15.8 million. However, based on data published by HHS, Blase estimated that this figure was by almost $11 billion higher and amounted to about $26.7 billion. It is probable that about 3 million households did not properly settle the accounts with the IRS for the benefits granted to them, whose average amount was about $525 higher than the amount to which the insured were entitled. This situation was caused by, for example: lack of taxpayers' awareness of the obligation to submit appropriate documents, high complexity of regulations related to APCT, too late settlement with the IRS, or lack of decisive action of the bureaucracy and not granting APTC to people who had not properly accounted for this issue with the IRS in previous years (Blase, 2016).

Death spiral Stage III – increase in the amount of out-of-pocket expenses

Rising premiums are not the only effect of the death spiral. Insurers also increase the level of deductible, co-payment, or co-insurance. These additional payments may vary depending on one's health plan. They are to prevent excessive consumption of medical services and to keep health insurance premiums at a relatively low level. Meanwhile, on the marketplaces/exchanges their growth is parallel to the increase in premiums, which causes difficulties for the insured who would like to benefit from certain medical services.

ObamaCare imposes a maximum limit on this type of payment, but they are still relatively higher than in the case of insurance concluded by the employer. In 2014, this limit was $6,350 for individual insurance and $12,700 for the family variant. In turn, in 2020, these values increased to $8,150 and $16,300, respectively (HealthCare.gov).

Generally, the main tool for limiting consumption among the insured is the deductible, that is, the amount that the insured must cover in the first place before the remaining expenses are covered by the insurance.[3] However, the amount of deductible between 2014–2020 systematically increased for all types of plans – except platinum, which covers no more than 1% of people. In turn, the deductible for the most popular silver plan increased from $2,425 in 2014 to $4,544 in 2020, which is an increase of 87% (KFF, 2019b).

Yet further data published by the Centres for Medicare & Medicaid Services, which also considers the amount of deductible with the support of the cost reduction program (CSR), shows that despite this, the amount of such expenses also increased for some insured people (Table 3.6). For the insured receiving CSR support at the level of 73%, the amount of their deductible in the years 2016–2020 increased by 21%. Slight decreases appeared in plans with CSR at the level of 87 and 94%, but they concern people with the lowest incomes (150–200% FPL; 100–150% FPL), where the maximum limit of direct expenses is much lower than in the case of the insured with higher incomes.[4]

These data clearly point to another significant problem related to ObamaCare, which is the fact that despite the support in the form of tax credits or CSR for many people, access to medical services remains problematic – even for people with relatively higher incomes, allocating several thousand dollars to direct spending is an insurmountable barrier. Although formally insured, they do not receive immediate access to medical services. It is also a spiral effect only regarding the increase in other payments than premiums. Furthermore, CSR is a denial or marginalization of the efforts of insurers trying to rationalize the excessive consumption of the insured resulting in a significant increase in premiums. It also shows that insurers are useful to the government only because it does not (yet) have its own institutional structures that can meet the goals set by ObamaCare. Thus, the government cooperates

Table 3.6 Average deductible including CSR for individual health plans in 2016–2020 (USD)

Year	Plan type		Average amount of deductible in the silver plan after considering CSR	Average deductible for all plans						
	Catastrophic	Bronze	Silver	73% CSR	87% CSR	94% CSR	Golden	Platinum	with CSR	without CSR
2016	6.850	5.923	3.049	2.586	609	160	966	222	2.142	4.275
2017	7.150	6.327	3.491	2.863	661	189	1.003	184	2.405	4.838
2018	7.350	6.153	3.970	2.945	710	231	1.243	146	2.685	4.972
2019	7.900	6.376	4.056	2.913	567	131	1.225	120	2.719	5.131
2020	8.150	6.446	4.181	3.128	517	105	1.319	101	2.835	5.316
Change %	19%	9%	37%	21%	-15%	-34%	37%	-55%	32%	24%

Source: Own study, based on: Centers for Medicare & Medicaid Services, 2020.

Note: Health plans from HealthCare.gov have been considered.

with the insurance industry, but introduces many regulations that distort its activities.

It is true that the level of these expenses can be shocking for many. However, this is not evidence of the market's unreliability but the result of the admission of many high-risk people to insurance, and the weakening of their price sensitivity. In addition, even supporters of ObamaCare admit that despite the reduction in premiums, a high level of, for example, deductible prevents them from taking advantage of the insurance. The media report many such cases. For instance, the *New York Times* cites the example of an insured person with a deductible of $6,500, which makes her visit the doctor less often than when she did not have insurance because then she could take advantage of the discount granted to the uninsured, which is now impossible. Another example is a 43-year-old Baltimore resident with family insurance. While his monthly premium is $275, the $13,000 deductible makes it impossible for his family to take advantage of the recommended benefits, especially for his son diagnosed with autism (Goodnough et al., 2020).

Although these cases may seem shocking and controversial, were it not for the high levels of deductible, and so on, premiums would have increased even more. It can be proven by the events of October 2017, when President Donald Trump decided to suspend payments under the CSR program because Congress had not allocated funds for this type of expenditure. Even earlier, since 2014, the legitimacy of this type of spending had been questioned by the United States House of Representatives (Department of Health and Human Services, 2017). This meant big problems for insurers, as in 2016 they received about $7 million under CSR, and in 2017 the number of insured covered by this program amounted to 7 million (58%) (Commonwealth Fund, 2017). According to Kaiser Family Foundation (KFF) estimates, insurers would have to raise premiums by an average of 19%[5] to compensate for the lost revenue. The forecasted scope of premium increases ranged from 9% (North Dakota) to 27% (Mississippi) (KFF, 2017). The increase in the premiums related to the suspension of CSR is referred to as silver loading because it concerns silver plans.

Furthermore, insurers went legal and began suing the federal government for withholding CSR payments. These cases found their way to the Federal Claims Court, and the first one began in

November 2017. In one case, an October 2019 court ruling stated that about 100 insurers were owed $1.6 billion for lost CSR revenue for 2017 and 2018. These cases are complex and the federal government in such situations appeals to the Court of Appeals for the Federal Circuit, where several such cases are already pending. As it turns out, in cases related to CSR, the ongoing proceedings regarding risk corridors also play an important role because, while making their decisions regarding CSR, the judges rely heavily on the federal district court of appeal's decisions on failing to meet the federal government's compensation for insurers from risk corridors (Keith, 2019).

To counteract the increasing problems related to silver loading, administrative actions were also taken. According to a statement from the Centers for Medicare & Medicaid Services, in 2020 the User Fee charged on insurance premiums sold on marketplaces/exchanges were reduced. The Federally facilitated Exchange (FFE) fee was reduced from 3.5% to 3% of the premium, while the fee for insurance sold through State-based Exchanges on the Federal Platform (SBE-FP) decreased from 3% to 2.5%. According to CMS, these fees were previously passed on to the consumer in the form of higher premiums, and their reduction is expected to bring the opposite result (Centers for Medicare & Medicaid Services, n. d.).

The problems with the increasing amount of deductible, and so on, also demonstrate why the phenomenon of underinsurance is increasingly gaining attention. According to The Commonwealth Fund report, the percentage of adults (19–64 years old) insured throughout the year who are also underinsured[6] is increasing – in 2014 it was 23%, and in 2018 it was 29%. In the case of insurance concluded by the employer, this percentage increased from 20% (2014) to 28% (2018), and for people insured individually (including on exchanges/markets) 42% (2018) (Fox & Brod, 2019).

Interestingly, according to The Commonwealth Fund, appropriate actions to be taken to counter the growing percentage of underinsured people include: expanding Medicaid; abolishing the 400% FPL limit entitling to receiving a tax credit; creating state or federal reinsurance programs to reduce premiums; increasing the limit of income entitling to receive CSR; excluding more medical services from deductible under all health plans; increasing the required minimum value covered by the employer (currently it is

60%). In addition, the authors of the proposals for these changes believe that policymakers should pay attention to the rising cost of health care (Fox & Brod, 2019).

From an economic point of view, some of the recommendations mentioned above are to continue the path to a single-payer system and socialized medicine. All these recommendations are to abolish part of the expenses incurred by the insured. Some of them are also a continuation of already invalid programs under ObamaCare. They seem to be right considering the context of increasing premiums and other expenses charged to the insured. However, the history of the US health care system has shown that it is the attempts to *cover the payments for* Americans in the context of medical services that lead to these negative effects.

Death spiral stage IV – decrease in the number of the insured

Not only did ObamaCare fail to attract enough people to the marketplaces/exchanges, and those who registered on them had to experience significant increases in premiums and other payments, but the number of people already insured began to fall. The largest number of people covered by insurance was recorded in 2016 – 12.7 million people. Later, their number gradually began to decrease, reaching 11.4 million people in 2020. Since the peak of 2016, the number of the insured therefore fell by 10%. Interestingly, these declines covered only federal marketplaces/exchanges, while in state ones the number of the insured remained unchanged (Figure 3.3).

Surprisingly, each of these values significantly deviates from the CBO estimates from previous years. For instance, in 2012 and 2014 the CBO assumed that in 2017 about 24–25 million people would be insured on the marketplaces/exchanges (Whitehouse.gov, 2017) but, as it turned out a few years later, there were only 12.2 million of them, which was not even half of the assumed target (48.8%). This is not accidental because, in principle, all such estimates published by the CBO were too optimistic (Figure 3.4).

Perhaps CBO assumed that the requirement to have insurance would prove to be an effective way to create a sufficiently large group of the insured. However, despite financial penalties many people remained uninsured. First, they ignored this obligation because in the past having insurance had been a voluntary

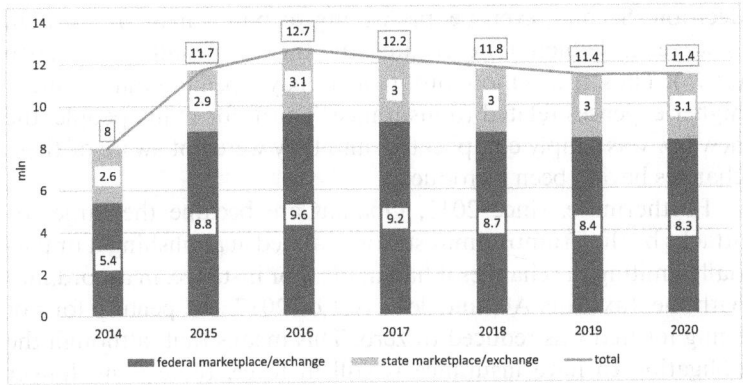

Figure 3.3 The number of the insured in federal and state marketplaces/ exchanges in the years 2014–2020

Source: Own study, based on: Centers for Medicare & Medicaid Services, 2020; Centers for Medicare & Medicaid Services, 2017.

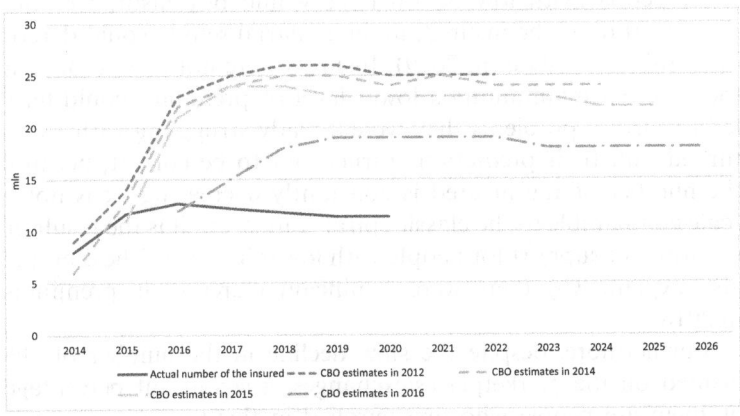

Figure 3.4 CBO estimates of the number of the insured on the marketplaces/exchanges and the actual state of affairs

Note: Estimates are for people under age 65.

Source: Own study, based on CBO estimates in particular years on the number of the insured in particular categories: (Estimates for the Insurance Coverage Provisions of the Affordable Care Act Updated for the Recent Supreme Court Decision; The Budget and Economic Outlook: 2014 to 2024; Insurance Coverage Provisions of the Affordable Care Act— CBO's March 2015 Baseline; Federal Subsidies for Health Insurance Coverage for People Under Age 65: Tables from CBO's March 2016 Baseline).

decision. Second, even people willing to buy it had to face high costs (e.g., deductible) exceeding the highest penalty as of 2016 ($695). Thus, it was more profitable to pay a penalty than to incur higher expenses related to insurance. Third, for many people, the new law was simply complicated, and they were not aware of these changes having been introduced.

Furthermore, since 2017, ObamaCare became the target of attacks by the Trump administration, aimed at abolishing it or partially limiting the changes it had made. For instance, in accordance with the Tax Cuts Act and Jobs Act of 2017, the penalty for not being insured was reduced to zero. This means that, although the obligation to have insurance is still in force, there is no longer any penalty for not meeting this requirement (these regulations have been in force since 2019). The exception is five states (DC, Massachusetts, New Jersey, California, and Rhode Island), where such penalties have been upheld (Norris, 2020b).

Although this regulation came into force in January 2019, insurers had already started to raise premiums for fear that fewer people with low health risks would buy insurance, and the structure of the insured, in an actuarial sense, would deteriorate (Simmons-Duffin, 2019). Insurers were not certain of it at the time but maintaining a lower level of premiums could have led to further problems they were already struggling with. As it turned out, their predictions turned out to be correct, because the number of the insured is constantly decreasing. It is not a scale comparable to the classic spiral course, but it is the result of government support for people with lower incomes. These events also explain why there were significant increases in premiums in 2018.

Furthermore, despite the slow decline in the number of the insured on the marketplaces/exchanges, a significant percentage of them are people who first enrolled in this type of insurance in a given year. For instance, in 2017, the number of the insured amounted to 12.2 million people and was 0.5 million lower than a year earlier (12.7 million). This does not mean, however, that 0.5 million people resigned from insurance. The total number of the newly registered on the marketplaces/exchanges amounted to 3.8 million and accounted for as much as 31% of the total 12.2 million insured people. Thus, in 2017 as many as 4.3 million people resigned from this type of insurance, that is, 34% of all the insured

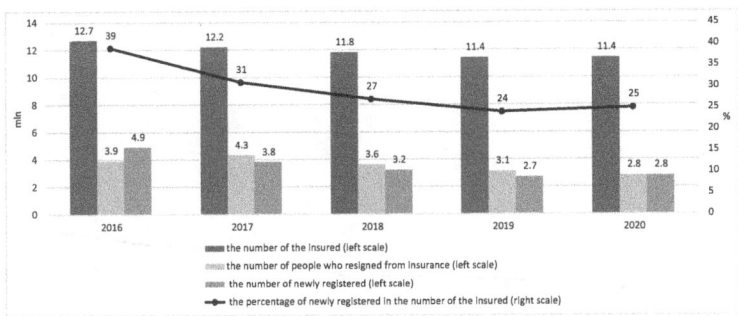

Figure 3.5 Newly insured on marketplaces/exchanges in individual years

Note: The data includes 50 states and the District of Columbia.

Source: Own study, based on: Centers for Medicare & Medicaid Services, 2020; Centers for Medicare & Medicaid Services, 2018; Centers for Medicare & Medicaid Services, 2017.

in 2016. Therefore, while the total number of the insured remains relatively stable, their turnover results significant (Figure 3.5).

To a large extent, a given level of the number of the insured is, therefore, maintained by new people registering for chosen plans. However, it can also be seen that after some time (a year or a few years later) there are numerous departures, which, in the absence of a sufficient number of new insured people, negatively affects the prospects for the stability of this type of programme. The number of new registrations has lost its dynamics, and since 2016, a smaller and smaller number of the insured has been recorded, which further distances ObamaCare from achieving its objectives.

Another issue is that some people in the face of increased costs may also switch from a more expensive plan to a cheaper one while maintaining the status of an insured person. For instance, in 2017, 71% of all the insured were covered by the silver plan, and 23% of them chose the more modest bronze plan. In turn, in 2020, the proportions were 59% and 33%, respectively, while the share of people enrolled in the golden plan increased from 4% to 7%. It turns out that some of the insured have a narrower scope of insurance coverage compared to a few years earlier (Figure 3.6).

One of the reasons explaining the current problems with low registration may also be the big problems encountered by the government website HealthCare.gov during the first registrations at

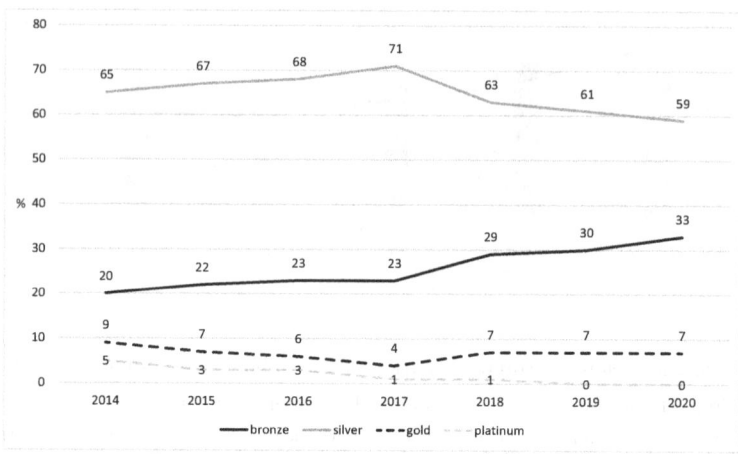

Figure 3.6 Percentage of the number of the insured in individual health plans

Note: The data includes 50 states and the District of Columbia. Individual values may not add up to their full values due to rounding them off and failure to consider catastrophic plans, whose share in 2014 amounted to 2% and in other years 1%.

Source: Own study, based on: the Department of Health and Human Services' annual publications on the number of insured persons in marketplaces/exchanges (Health Insurance Marketplace: Summary Enrolment Data for the Initial Annual Open Enrolment Period).

the end of 2013. The problems with its functionality were visible from the beginning of its launch, that is, from 1 October. The number of visits to the website turned out to be five times higher than assumed and after 2 hours it stopped working. As a result, on the first day of registration, only six users managed to fill in their applications and choose their health plan. The situation started to change after the website's bandwidth was improved (Harvard Business School, 2016).

Undoubtedly, the confusion associated with the website failure had some effect on the fact that in 2014 only 5.4 million people were insured with the help of HealthCare.gov. On Harvard Business School's technology website devoted to technologies and operation management one can read about the main reasons that were behind the malfunction of the site. They are detailed and described in Table 3.7.

Table 3.7 Causes of HealhCare.gov malfunction

---

1. **Lack of experience**
   The people employed to implement the project had relevant experience in insurance markets or servicing large government projects, but they lacked experience in the implementation of technological projects. Important technical positions were not filled, and the managers of individual projects did not have adequate knowledge, which resulted in a small amount of time spent on testing and solving technical problems with the site.

2. **Lack of leadership and proper management**
   There was no formal division of tasks among multiple units, which led to delays in making key decisions or lack of proper communication. For example, a contractor dealing with a login system estimated the low demand for this type of function, because at the beginning it was assumed that it was possible to insure oneself without creating an account and logging in. However, technical delays meant that the implementation of this idea did not continue, which meant that all users had to go through the login stage. However, the bandwidth was not increased.

3. **Pressure**
   Since ObamaCare went into effect, HHS employees were pressured to launch the site on time, regardless of the stage of work, the number of the problem-solving tests conducted and their results.

Source: Own study, based on: Harvard Business School, 2016.

The problems described in Table 3.7 led to an increase in spending on solving problems with the functionality of the website. As a result, the initial budget of the project increased from $93.7 million to $1.7 billion. Interestingly, the failure to implement HealthCare.gov is nothing new because, according to research, in the previous 10 years, as many as 94% of large federal IT projects had failed. More than half of them were delayed, exceeded the budget, or did not meet the expectations. In addition, about 41% of such projects were considered complete failures (Harvard Business School, 2016).

Death spiral stage V – unreliability of insurers' support

In addition to problems with the falling number of the insured, insurers also had to face a shortage of funds from support programs specially created for them: the reinsurance program and risk corridors.

In the case of the former, the surplus of funds was reached only for 2014, when (in 2015) CMS reported that the total amount of payments was $9.7 billion with claims (payments) of $7.9 billion. Therefore, it was possible to cover 100% of the claims and the surplus of $1.7 billion was transferred to the next year. In turn, the estimated payments for 2015 amounted to $6.5 billion, but the claims submitted by insurers were already more than twice as high – $14.3 billion, which shows that they were already better understood by the risk assessment specialists. It is also important that $0.5 billion of the amount raised (in the form of a surplus of more than $6 billion) had to be transferred to the United States Department of the Treasury as an operating cost of the program. Thus, considering the surplus in 2014, approximately $7.8 billion was raised, representing approximately 55.1% of the value of claims for 2015 (Centers for Medicare & Medicaid Services, 2016). The deficit of funds also occurred in the last year of this programme, in 2016. The amount of funds raised was approximately $3.96 billion, which accounted for 52.9% of the total claims of $7.5 billion. Thus, it was almost half the amount compared to 2015, but it resulted mainly from the increase in the payment threshold (from $45,000 to $90,000) above which part of the insurers' expenses was covered. It also further evidences how high health risk is represented by people insured on the marketplaces/exchanges. Importantly, most payers are also beneficiaries of this programme. For instance, in 2015 such support was received by 497 (86%) of all 575 entities, and in 2016 it was 445 (89%) of 496 in total (Centers for Medicare & Medicaid Services, 2016).

The risk corridor program did not provide insurers with the expected support either. According to CMS estimates, total claims under this program for 2014 amounted to $2.87 billion, and the collected funds from insurers' premiums were only $362 million, or 12.6% of total claims. This difference was to be covered by future premiums and government funds. It was consistent with the initial assumptions, but already in 2014 CMS announced that this program was to be budget neutral. Then, in 2015, HHS reported that under the neutrality principle, it could only pay out about $240 million of nearly $3 billion in claims. Additionally, the Republican-controlled Congress passed a legislation to block CMS from acting to allocate general funds to insurers (Cox et al., 2016b).

Dissatisfied with such an unfavourable development, insurers began to demand compensation for their losses and sue the federal government. One such case eventually went to the Supreme Court, which, based on its April 2020 ruling, ordered the payment of \$12 billion to four insurers (Moda Health, Maine Community Health Options, Land of Lincoln Mutual Insurance Co., and Blue Cross Blue Shield of North Carolina) as part of the 2014–2016 risk corridor program. According to the Court, the government was obliged to make such payments even in the absence of a clear definition of the allocation of funds. The federal government's efforts, therefore, halted these payments in the short term, but they did not absolve its responsibility in the long term (Keith, 2020).

It is important for insurers because one of the reasons for expanding their activities to marketplaces/exchanges was the government's promise to cover the remaining losses, which was to keep premiums at a stable level. Therefore, the Supreme Court's decision may have had some impact on the reduction of premiums in the following years for some health plans. Another serious consequence of this decision may be further rulings in favour of insurers in other pending cases of this type, or further lawsuits. In ongoing cases, insurers are demanding additional billions of dollars from the federal government, as in one class-action lawsuit involving at least 116 insurers expecting more than \$12 billion in outstanding payments, the case is in the Federal Court of Claims. In another case, the Health Care Service Corporation, which serves Blue Cross Blue Shield plans in five states, sued the government for more \$2 billion in unpaid payments under risk corridors (Keith, 2020).

The suspension of this type of payment can be attributed to political issues, and so on, but regardless of them, even a cursory analysis shows that the payments demanded by insurers were underestimated by the government – hence, among other things, the efforts to limit them. These programs could only fulfil their purpose if the profits of some insurers resulted from the losses of others, and this is not the effect of market exchange.

Death spiral stage VI – insurers' losses and exits from Healthcare Insurance Marketplaces

The losses that insurance companies began to incur prompted some of them to leave at least some of the state marketplaces/

exchanges. As was the case with the first reported premium increases, exit decisions were announced by large and experienced insurers such as UnitedHealth Group, Aetna, and Humana. The main factors that influenced their decisions include high health risk of the insured, too few insured people with lower risk, or problems with covering losses from government sources. An additional difficulty was also the regulations prohibiting the sale of health plans between state borders, which undoubtedly made it difficult to balance the risk.

In April 2016, the largest health insurer in the USA, UnitedHealth Group, announced that by the end of 2017 it would leave most of the state marketplaces/exchanges where it insured nearly 800,000 people, remaining in 4 out of the 16 states (Michigan, Oklahoma, Arkansas, and parts of Georgia). The insurer estimated its losses for 2016 alone at about $650 million. Interestingly, representatives of the United States Department of Health and Human Services found that the plans offered by UnitedHealth were usually more expensive than those offered by competitors (Kodiak, 2016). They forget, however, that the insured for some reason chose these more expensive insurances and soon they would be forced to choose a less satisfactory solution.

A few months later, another major insurer – Aetna – also announced its planned exit from 11 out of 15 states in which it had been present until then. The insurer would continue to offer individual insurance in this dozen or so states, but outside the marketplaces/exchanges because there were too many people with high health risks. Aetna estimated its losses for 2016 at $300 million. This decision means that about 80% of Aetna's 838,000 customers in 2017 will have to change their insurance (Tracer, 2016). However, as Mark Bertolini, CEO of Aetna, stated (Tracer, 2016):

> Most payers experience constant financial stress as part of their activities on the marketplaces/exchanges. Providing consumers with affordable, high-quality healthcare options is not possible without a balanced risk pool.

Even more radical steps were taken by another insurer – Humana – which at the beginning of 2017 announced that by 2018 it would completely abandon the offer of individual health insurance, including those offered on marketplaces/exchanges. As the main reason for this decision, the insurer cites the inability to effectively manage the costs of ill patients due to an unsustainable risk pool. Humana insured around 150,000 people in 2017. The insurer reduced its activity in this type of markets gradually: in 2016 it operated in 15 states, and in 2017 only in 11. Another important reason for this decision was the federal judge's blocking of the possibility of a merger with Aetna as part of better cost consolidation (Japsen, 2017).

This is the aftermath of the strong position of the Department of Justice, which is trying to block such transactions, invoking antitrust laws. Previously four insurers (Aetna and Humana, and Anthem and Cigna) announced its willingness to merge to better manage costs in the marketplaces/exchanges. These two mergers were to bring these entities greater stability of their operations, which would also be beneficial for their clients. However, the Justice Department filed a lawsuit against these transactions, arguing that their completion would lead to higher prices and lower competition (Bartz, 2017). In January 2017, Aetna's proposal to acquire Humana for $34 billion was blocked by the US District Court, and in February the same fate befell the planned merger worth $54 billion between Anthem and Cigna (US Department of Justice, 2017).

Many smaller entities also had problems staying on the marketplaces/exchanges. An alternative and additional competition for commercial insurers were to be smaller entities – the so-called health cooperatives (co-ops). They functioned as non-profit organizations with their members on the board. As a rule, they were to be consumer- rather than profit-oriented and offer cheaper health plans than their commercial competitors (Galewitz, 2016).

Twenty-three cooperatives were created, and they additionally received a total of $2.4 billion in loans from the federal government to start operations. According to the government, such support was received by entities that were able to demonstrate adequate financial stability in the future. The efforts of the federal government should come as no surprise, because these 23 cooperatives were a kind of *replacement* for the previously planned so-called *public option* – health insurance managed by the government, whose creation ultimately did not occur (Pipes, 2016).

However, as it turned out, cooperatives had problems with maintaining financial stability from the beginning of their activity.

To limit the losses, they undertook, among other things, attempts to renegotiate contracts with hospitals and other suppliers. Despite these efforts, their numbers quickly began to decrease. At the beginning of their activity, they insured about 1 million Americans, but in 2017 there were only 7 cooperatives on the market (out of 23) cooperatives insuring 350,000 people (Galewitz, 2016). The 16 cooperatives that were closed received $1.7 billion in government support.

According to the Inspector General of the Department of Health and Human Services report from July 2015, all but one of the cooperatives suffered losses and more than half of them reported net losses of at least $15 million in its first year of operation. Furthermore, the report also drew attention to the fact that many of them set premiums at a higher level than commercial insurers (Levinson/Department of Health and Human Services – Office of the Inspector General, 2015).

The reasons for cooperatives' poor financial condition and their collapse include such factors as: inadequate risk assessment process, too few insured, too many insured with high health risk, or inadequate management. Moreover, cooperatives had to face a lack of government support from the risk corridor program. Another problem was the complex risk adjustment mechanism, which required cooperatives to pay additional expenses. For instance, under ObamaCare's risk adjustment program, HealthlyCT had to pay an additional $13.4 million, which significantly impaired its financial stability. Another Oregon health cooperative, after reporting an $18 million loss in 2015, expected $5 million in support from this program, but instead received an additional bill of $0.9 million. In turn, the Land of Lincoln co-operation ended 2015 with a $91 million loss but was required to pay additional $32 million. It should come as no surprise, then, that so many of them ceased to operate, and some began to sue the federal government for lack of support (risk corridors) and the requirement to make unjustified (according to the cooperative) payments to the risk adjustment program (Pipes, 2016).

Despite the considerable support of the government, all these factors led to the collapse of such initiatives. At the end of 2020, another health cooperative – New Mexico Health Connections (19,000 insured in 2019) – was closed, which meant that in 2021 their number shrank to 3 from the initial 23 in 2014. These other three cooperatives in 2019 covered a total of about 107,000 people (Norris, 2020a).

In the face of the above problems faced by both larger and smaller entities, their total number began to gradually decrease. In 2015, there were an average of 6 insurers per state marketplace/exchange, and in 2018 only 3.5. In the following years, the situation began to somewhat improve (Figure 3.7).

However, it should be emphasized that the market was abandoned by some of the larger insurers, which is worrying. In turn, the entities remaining on the market had to significantly increase premiums and other fees such as, for example, deductibles. Therefore, the situation is not stabilized, especially when it became clear that it had not been possible to attract enough young people to adequately distribute the risk among the different groups.

In addition to higher spending, the insured who remained on the marketplaces/exchanges also had less choice when it came to health plans – in 2020, 32% of them could choose their health plans between one (10%) or two (22%) insurers. This is still an improvement compared to 2018, when 32% of the insured could take advantage of the offer of only one insurer, and another 32%

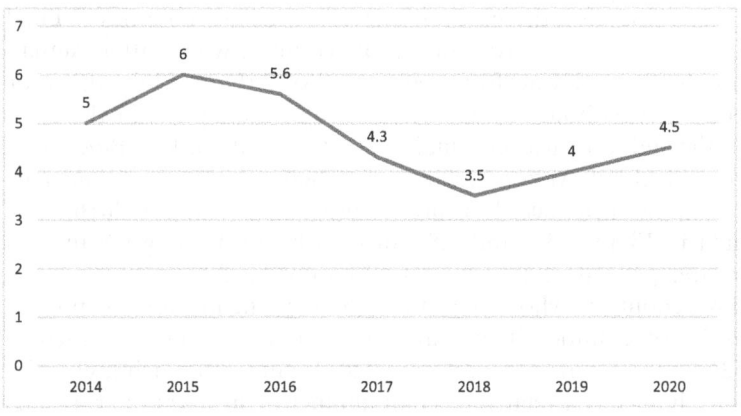

Figure 3.7 Average number of insurers in each state offering health plans through the Healthcare Insurance Marketplaces

Note: The data comes from HealthCare.gov and from the data provided by given states.

Source: Own study, based on: Fehr et al., 2019.

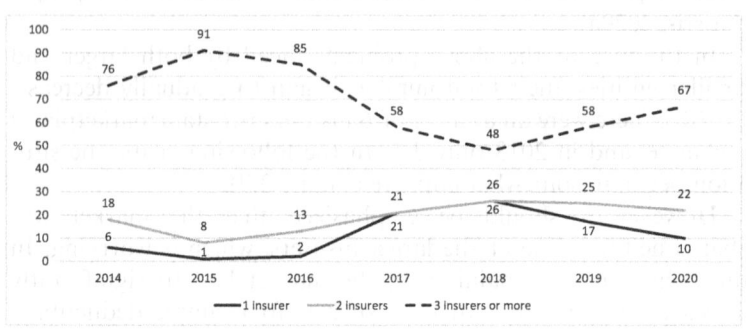

Figure 3.8 The share of the insured (in per cent) having access to a certain number of insurers offering health plans as part of the
Healthcare Insurance Marketplaces

Note: The data comes from HealthCare.gov and from the data provided by given
states. The data may not add up to 100% due to rounding the numbers off.

Source: Own study, based on: Fehr et al., 2019.

could choose between two of them (Figure 3.8); this was the result
of, among other things, exits of larger insurers and bankruptcies
of smaller entities.

There is also the case of one of Arizona's counties – Pinal
County – known across the whole country, which after Aetna's
decision to withdraw from the state as of 2017 faced the threat of
being left without any insurer offering health plans in the area.
In the end, one insurer remained on the local market (Blue Cross
Blue Shield of Arizona), allowing 10,000 insured to continue participating in the health insurance program (Alltucker, 2016). The
data in Figures 3.7 and 3.8 can be a bit misleading because an
insurer present in a given state does not have to offer insurance
throughout the whole area. In 2016, only one insurer was present
in 7% of counties. Two years later, this percentage increased to
52%, and amounted to 25% in 2020 (Figure 3.9). Such high vola-
tility indicates a relatively small number of insurers offering specific health plans. Thus, even the exit of one of them can cause
serious fluctuations in each marketplace/exchange.

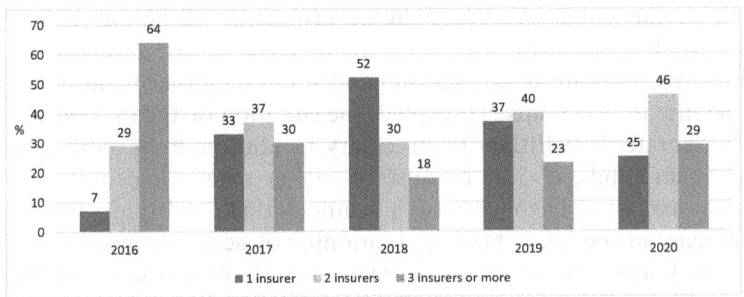

Figure 3.9 The number of counties (in per cent) with a certain number of insurers

Note: The data comes from HealthCare.gov and from the data provided by given states.

Source: Own study, based on: Fehr, et al., 2019; Fehr et al., 2018; Cox et al., 2016a.

Conclusion

The marketplaces/exchanges created did not make it easier for Americans to access affordable health care and proved to be volatile. Based on the above analysis, it is impossible to indicate a group that would be satisfied and calm about their future. The case of the creation and functioning of marketplaces/exchanges demonstrates how complex the insurance market is and that government's efforts to regulate it did not bring the expected results. The death spiral initiated by ObamaCare regulations has a slightly different course, but its negative consequences are felt by all market/exchange participants: the insured, insurers, state governments, and the federal government.

The future of this project is not optimistic for several reasons. First, the departures of some insurers, although beneficial for them, have left some people with high health risks without insurance. Some of these people have chosen other health plans, which soon may lead to further increases in premiums and to further destabilization of health plans. In other words: such people may generate similar or even higher costs for subsequent insurers. Second, insurers are not obliged to participate in such markets, so in the event of further losses, some of them may act similarly to UnitedHealth, Aetna, or Humana. Third, if further increases in premiums are reported, state governments will be put against the wall. If they do not accept the increases, more insurers will leave the state marketplaces/exchanges. On the other hand, if the increase in premiums is accepted, the situation of the insured will deteriorate. It will then be necessary to allocate even more government funds, if only because of higher relief for people with lower incomes. Therefore, it is a deadlock that will bring a further increase in spending, taxes and rationing of access to medical services. Fourth, insurers were overly optimistic about the possibility of offering these kinds of affordable health plans. Government support programs also failed, which means that in the future they may be more distant from this type of cooperation. Fifth, insurers cannot operate on a market basis – they only act as intermediaries operating within the rigid framework created by the ObamaCare regulations. The involvement of the federal government, both from the fiscal and regulatory side, is high. However, in the future it may increase when it turns out that insurers will no longer want to be present on the marketplaces/exchanges. This situation may lead to the creation of completely government-controlled health insurance options/plans without the participation of private entities.

Private health insurance market

Individual health insurance market outside marketplaces/exchanges

Significant changes were also introduced into the individual health insurance market, where about 14 million people had been insured before ObamaCare. Some of them made this choice due to running their own businesses or due to the lack of insurance offered by their employers. Some opted for individual insurance also because of the desire to choose a catastrophic plan with a limited scope, lower premium, and higher own costs.

After ObamaCare was passed, it became clear that these health plans would have to go through an adjustment process to comply with the reform assumptions – for example, because of the scope of insurance. Naturally, this sparked growing concerns among the insured about the future of their health plans which they wanted to keep unchanged. President Obama also tried to alleviate the situation by repeatedly assuring that everyone would be able to keep their individual plans if they wished to do so. However, it soon turned out impossible. Maintaining older plans in their unchanged form could significantly hinder the achievement of the assumed goals, because too few people would choose to buy insurance on the marketplaces/exchanges due to the existence of cheaper options, and so on. This, in turn, gave rise to (legitimate) concerns about the appropriate distribution of risk or insurance costs to individual groups.

Bearing in mind the pressure to preserve these health plans, it was decided to leave some of them, even though they did not fully meet the requirements set by ObamaCare. These plans were referred to as grandfathered plans, and the condition for their preservation was their conclusion at the latest by 23 March 2010. However, according to preliminary estimates, about 70% of such insurance was to be cancelled, which further increased the pressure to maintain the possibility of their continuation. Such a large scale of cancellations resulted from the fact that the requirements set by the creators of the changes were rigorous, for example, regarding the scope of insurance, which in the case of individual policies was usually more limited. Furthermore, several problems emerged in the case of preserved health plans. First, these were the so-called block closure plans, which meant that new insured people could not be admitted to them. Such insurance would become more and more expensive over time due to the aging group of the insured or possible early resignations of some of them, which in their case may cause further small death spirals. These plans would sooner or later have to be withdrawn by insurers anyway. Second, even for some of those insurers who were willing to continue with their previous health plans, a significant obstacle was the stringent requirements as to the insurance coverage, provider network, premiums, and so on. Even minor modifications could lead to the loss of *inherited* insurance status.

All these factors drove many insurers to cancel at least some of their existing health plans to propose new options which would be aligned with ObamaCare requirements. For instance, Florida Blue cancelled about 300,000 of its individual health plans, which accounted for 80% of all their plans in the state. Kaiser Permanente withdrew 160,000 policies in California, which accounted for 50% of their plans in the area in total. Another California insurer, Blue

Shield of California, sent about 119,000 cancellation letters to its customers, which accounted for 60% of their individual health plans. In addition, the insurer informed that about two-thirds of the insured should expect premium increases. Independence Blue Cross withdrew 45% of their health plans in Philadelphia, and Highmark cancelled 20% in Pennsylvania (Appleby & Gorman, 2013).

Interestingly, the last two insurers cancelled the health plans of the insured with already existing medical conditions. In turn, the insured with lower health risks were offered to extend their insurance for another year. Hence, insurers were suspected of wanting to redirect the insured to marketplaces/exchanges and improve the risk structure of the insured in their individual plans (Appleby & Gorman, 2013). Regardless of the legitimacy of these suspicions, the actions of insurers should not be surprising. If there is no way for them to reduce the costs, they must take more decisive actions to retain at least some of their existing customers. Otherwise, such insurance would become too expensive for the latter group of the insured, and it would be the latter group that would be forced to give up such insurance.

According to the Urban Institute estimates, at the end of 2013 cancellations involved about 2.6 million individual health plans, which accounted for 18.6% of this market. Due to multiple complaints, in November of the same year the Department of Health and Human Services allowed states to continue with non-ObamaCare compliant insurance in 2014,[7] and later extended this period to 2017 (in the end, 40 states took advantage of this option) (Clemans-Cope & Anderson, 2015). However, after this period, it was decided to further extend such health plans. A bulletin published by CMS in March 2019 provided further guidance allowing states to extend these plans for 2021[8]. According to them, states would be able to decide whether the extension was to last for the whole year or part of it, and whether the extension was to cover the individual market or also small group markets (Centers for Medicare & Medicaid Services, 2019a).

In addition, the status of *inherited plans* is also granted to some group insurances concluded by the employer. Like in the case of individual insurance, these are health plans that were already in effect at the time ObamaCare was enacted but did not meet all the requirements of the act. These plans could be continued if companies did not significantly change the costs distribution, the premiums, or the scope of insurance. New employees may join such insurance if the company had continuously provided such an opportunity. According to data from the Kaiser Family Foundation, in 2019, 22% of all companies offered their employees at least one inherited health plan, which covered 13% of all insured employees. Interestingly, as many as 20% of all employees/ representatives of state or local governments have *inherited* health plans, which is the second highest percentage (after the wholesale industry – 25%), considering the division into individual parts (industries) of the US economy (KFF, 2019c).

Cadillac Tax

Employers offering health insurance to their employees experienced great uncertainty related to the prospect of imposing a tax on high-cost health plans. Its implementation was postponed several times, most recently to 2022. Finally, on 20 December 2019, President Trump signed a bill completely abolishing its entry into force. Many employers, trade unions, insurers, and others were opposed to the new tax. It was feared that to avoid it (or delay) employers would limit the scope of insurance, increase employee costs (e.g., deductible), or compensate for the costs of the new tax by reducing employees' wages (Cigna, 2019).

Furthermore, its introduction would require clarification of many details. For instance, the limit on the premium above which tax was to be charged in 2022 was estimated at $11,000 for individual policies and $30,000 for policies in the family variant. However, these limits were to be increased for the insured performing high-risk occupations such as, for example, law enforcement or construction work. Higher limits were also to cover some groups of the insured, depending on their demographic structure (including age and gender). The tax was also to cover savings accumulated in medical savings accounts, so that employers would not transfer funds saved on, for example, reductions in premiums. The amount of tax was to increase along with the premium (Table 3.8) (Cigna).

According to Kaiser Family Foundation estimates, the new tax would cover about 21% of employers offering health insurance if it took effect in 2022. This percentage would increase to 31% if voluntary employee contributions to Flexible Spending

Table 3.8 Examples of Cadillac Tax rates – if it had come into effect
in 2018

Individual insurance					
Health plan cost (USD)	11,000	12,000	13,000	14,000	15,000
Tax (USD)	320	720	1,120	1,520	1,920
Family variant insurance					
Health plan cost (USD)	28,000	30,000	32,000	34,000	36,000
Tax (USD)	200	1,000	1,800	2,600	3,400

Source: Own study, based on: Cigna.

Note: The limits above which the 40% tax is charged are from 2018 and amount to $10,200 for the individual variant and $27,500 for the family variant. In 2022, they were to be increased.

The health plan cost includes premiums paid by both the employer and the employee. However, it does not include direct expenses covered by employees such as deductibles, co-payment, or co-insurance.

Accounts – accounts operating on a similar principle as medical savings accounts – were also included. It is worth noting, however, that these estimates assume that employers will not modify their health plans to avoid taxation (KFF, 2019a).

Before the abolition of this tax, companies took actions aiming at reducing costs below the thresholds set. However, according to CFOs, these actions could not have been expected to be effective because of lack of sufficient information from the US Treasury Department and the Tax Office. Therefore, decisions were made in conditions of great uncertainty. For instance, one of the companies – Adaptive Biotechnologies – to reduce spending on health services, planned to change the form of insurance from one offered and administered by the insurer (fully insured) for self-insured. In turn, according to the CFO of Brookfield Infrastructure Partners LP – a company offering energy services – the only solution was to transfer costs to employees. Therefore, the decision to repeal the announced tax was received with great approval. Previously, an initiative called *The Alliance to Fight the 40* was also created, bringing together over 1,000 public and private entities and institutions that sought the complete abolition of this tax. It included, among others, such entities as Exxon Mobil Corp, Pfizer Inc, or AT&T Inc, many trade unions and patient support organizations (Maurer, 2019).

In addition to the abolition of this tax, two other levies were also repealed: Health Insurer Tax and Medical Device Tax. The former would expire from 2021. The total revenue from these taxes in 2014 amounted to $8 million and was steadily growing. They depended on the market share of the insurer concerned. In turn, the latter tax of 2.3% covered revenues from the sale of medical devices. It was in force between 2013–2015 and was suspended in 2016–2019. As of 31 December 3 2019, it has been completely abolished (Cigna, 2019).

New obligations for 'big' employers

Despite the abolition of the individual mandate – the obligation to have health insurance – and several other taxes, some regulations remained in force. These included, for example, the obligation (since 2015/2016) for large employers to offer health plans with certain standards to their employees. The ObamaCare adjustments did not cause as much confusion in the employee insurance market as in the case of the individual market because employers' plans had a wider scope of insurance, among others.

However, for some companies the new regulations meant higher costs. Therefore, to avoid them, they could reduce the number of hours of at least part of their full-time employees, for example, from 35 to 29 or 28 hours a week. In this context, a new group of Americans was talked about – *the 29ers*, that is, employees affected by such reductions in working time (Henderson, 2016) because, If the company does not employ a minimum of 50 full-time employees, ObamaCare regulations will not cover it. Other possible effects include a reduction in the wages of full-time employees. ObamaCare is no exception – an employer cannot maintain the number of hours or adequate levels of employee pay while covering higher insurance costs unless their marginal work productivity increases accordingly.

Reducing employees' working hours can also have negative legal consequences. An example of this is the case of Dave & Buster's – an American restaurant and entertainment service chain – which was sued by its employees for reducing their working hours so that the company could avoid complying with ObamaCare requirements. This reduction entailed the loss of health insurance and full-time employee status. According to the employees, these actions violated the Employee Retirement Income Security Act (ERISA) and unlawfully deprived them of the health insurance they had had before ObamaCare went into effect in 2014 (Hawkins & Hwang, 2018).

The provisions of ERISA prevent employers from intentionally taking actions that may limit or hinder employees from receiving certain benefits. In turn, the company's management during several meetings with employees reported that the adjustments to the requirements of ObamaCare would generate more than $2 million additional costs, which the company wanted to avoid. Ultimately, a Federal Court judge approved the proposed $7.4 million monetary settlement which provided compensation for Dave & Buster's 1,200 current and former full-time employees (Sheen, 2020).

Part of the public may consider this a victory for employees and at the same time criticize the company's actions. However, in the long run, more similar court rulings (or even the possibility of similar outcomes) may prompt some employers to, for example, hire new employees only part-time to avoid potential lawsuits in the future. The cost of the settlement will also likely be (in part) compensated by Dave & Buster's in the form of lower salaries in the future, smaller investments, and so on. It is true that the situation of employees has deteriorated, but the main reason for this situation should be considered the ObamaCare regulations, which caused the company's specific actions. Reducing costs is an important factor in entrepreneurial activity and hindering such activities increases the companies' inefficiency, which leads to worse satisfaction of consumer needs. For instance, a company can make an erroneous investment and then save itself by partial job reductions. However, this case concerns a completely different situation – the desire to avoid additional and certain costs not resulting from changes in the market but from forced regulations. The rights of workers under specific laws in no way abolish economic rights and market principles.

Nonetheless, the regulations covering health insurance long before 2014 in some way had a negative impact on the labour market, for example, by limiting employees' mobility when they were less willing to change jobs or start their own businesses due to the fear of losing a convenient health plan or receiving its inferior version, and so on.

The greater nuisance of the new regulations for smaller employers may also help explain why in smaller companies (3–199 employees) as many as 19% of insured employees have inherited health plans, while in companies with 200 or more employees this percentage (in 2019) amounted to 10% (KFF, 2019c).

What is more, employers are burdened with additional administrative tasks because they must prove that they have offered their employees an Offer of Health Insurance in accordance with the requirements of ObamaCare in a given year. This confirmation consists of providing full-time employees with special forms, in a timely manner, and sending a copy of them to the IRS by regular mail or electronically if their number is 250 or more (Internal Revenue Service, b).

Pharmaceutical market

New perspectives for pharmaceutical companies

Along with the insurers, pharmaceutical companies also found themselves in a new reality. ObamaCare regulations imposed certain obligations and burdens, but also provided them with certain benefits. The former includes, for example, the government's desire to obtain larger discounts on prescription drugs for beneficiaries of programs such as Medicare (part D), Medicaid, or a new tax covering manufacturers and importers of original drugs. In turn, the assumed increase in the number of the insured on individual markets, or obligations imposed on employers, significantly increased the number of potential customers.

This influenced the positive forecasts for the growth prescription drugs (RX) sales, especially among the group of people up to 26 years of age who could use their parents' insurance longer, and for those insured through newly created marketplaces/exchanges which gave them a wide scope of insurance and covered the greater part of the costs for people with lower incomes (Daemmrich, 2011, pp. 28–29). According to data from the consulting and research firm Global Data from 2015, these conditions partly contributed to the higher forecast increase in the value of the pharmaceutical market in the USA from $395 billion in 2014 to $548 billion in 2020 (Drug Discovery Trends Editor, 2015). For manufacturers of original drugs, this is even more beneficial because the forecasted sales increases coincide with expiring patents for popular original drugs such as, for example, Lipitor (a drug lowering blood cholesterol) from Pfizer, Plavix (an antiplatelet drug) produced by Bristol-Myers Squibb, or the antidiabetic drug Actos manufactured by Eli Lilly and Takeda Pharmaceuticals (Japsen, 2013).

Higher discounts on prescription drugs

One of the goals of ObamaCare was to financially support seniors who found themselves in the so-called donut hole in buying medicines. In this aspect, several changes supporting the elderly in the purchase of prescription drugs had been implemented by 2020 in Medicare (Part D). In the first place, the insured allocates funds for the purchase of medicines from their own pocket up to $435 (deductible). After incurring these expenses, they proceed to the next stage (initial coverage period) in which the insurance covers most of the costs and the senior covers a smaller part of them through co-payment or co-insurance. When the total spending on medications funded by a given health plan and the insured reaches $4,020, they fall into a gap called a donut hole. Then the senior covers 25% of the cost of buying medicines, which is a relatively lower percentage than in previous years. For instance, when buying an additional medicine for $100, they must pay 25% of that amount, that is, $25. When the sum of the insured's total out-of-pocket expenses reaches $6,350, they are covered with the catastrophic coverage. In this last stage, their spending on subsequent drugs does not exceed 5% of the price of each of them or $3.60 for generic drugs and $8.95 for original drugs (whichever is higher) (Medicare Interactive).

Moreover, the limit from which catastrophic coverage applies increased significantly in 2020 – a year earlier it was $5,100, and in 2010 – $4,550. This means that the insured with higher expenses on RX drugs will stay in the donut hole longer. According to data from the KFF, in 2017 there were 4.9 million people in it, out of whom about a million achieved catastrophic coverage (KFF, 2019d).

Before ObamaCare, the insured people fell into a donut hole after exceeding $2,800 in spending (including a health plan). They then incurred 100% of their expenses until the $4,550 limit was reached. The changes moved the first threshold to $4,020 and reduced the share of the insured person's expenses to 25%

after exceeding it. However, this required pharmaceutical companies to be obliged to provide 50% discounts on drug purchases the moment the insured found themselves in the donut hole. According to estimates, the total amount of these discounts cost drug manufacturers more than $25 billion between 2011 and 2016. Moreover, as indicated by O'Neill Hayes of the American Action Forum, The Bipartisan Budget Act of 2018 increased their amount to 70% (from 2019) and extended their use to biosimilars, which will further increase the cost of these discounts (O'Neill Hayes, 2018). In 2018, approximately 42.5 million people were enrolled in Medicare (Part D) (Donohue & Huskamp, 2018, p. 1957).

Similar changes included another government program, Medicaid. Pharmaceutical companies wishing to sell their products under this program were required to offer *the best price* they offered to other payers or to provide a new permanent discount.[9] The amount of this discount (for original drugs) was significantly increased and amounted to 23.1% of their price (an increase of 53%). Manufacturers had to sell their drugs to almost 25% of the US population for about 75% of their price. The discounts granted under the Medicaid program in years 2011–2015 was estimated at $80 billion. The amount was also influenced by the expansion of Medicaid in many states, which further increased the number of beneficiaries (O'Neill Hayes, 2018).

Granting high discounts was not the only condition for pharmaceutical companies. For their drugs to be covered by the Medicaid program, they also had to participate in another discount program – the 340B Drug Pricing Program – which involved additional discounts on outpatient drugs covered by insurance. Their purchase is made by authorized medical institutions and then they find their way to eligible patients. The discount takes the form of a maximum price and is related to the amount of the Medicaid discount, which may lead to a situation where the price is zero or takes a negative value – then a price of one cent is set (O'Neill Hayes, 2018). The new regulations significantly increased the number of medical facilities eligible to receive this type of discount – until the ObamaCare enactment (March 2010), the number of such facilities did not exceed 4,000, but in 2011–2015 more than 19,000 of new facilities eligible for these discounts were registered. This led to an increase in sales of medicines under this program from $6.4 billion in 2011 to $16.2 billion in 2016 (O'Neill Hayes, 2018).

In addition to the discounts granted for the purchase of medicines, in 2011 a new tax on manufacturers and importers of original medicines came into force. In the years 2011–2019, manufacturers and importers of original medicines paid a total of more than $28 billion under the new tax (Internal Revenue Service, a).

Increase in drug prices

Pharmaceutical companies had to make considerable concessions to offer their products under government insurance programs, which affected their revenues and profits. A certain problem turned out to be a lower than assumed number of the insured on the marketplaces/exchanges, that is, where such discounts did not apply. It should come as no surprise, then, that these new conditions – at least in part – may have contributed to an increase in the prices of drugs that included, for example, people insured by Medicare (Part D). If a company must give a significant discount on its product expressed as a percentage of the drug's price, then, for example, to partially compensate for the lost revenue, it will increase the price of the drug for seniors from $100 to $150, and so on. The amount of the discount will still be 70%, but of a higher price.

Noticeable increases in drug prices occurred in the first years after ObamaCare was signed or went into effect. Attention was drawn to, for example, cases of original prescription drugs whose prices increased by an average of more than 40% between October 2012 and April 2015, which was 13 times higher than the inflation rate (e.g., Lipitor – 51%; Norvasc – 46%) (Belk, 2016).

According to the IMS Institute for Healthcare Informatics, the average price of original prescription drugs increased by 17.0% in 2013 and by 24.9%. in 2014, while the average price of generics increased by 2.9% and 9.8% respectively, in these two years. The fees resulting from the new tax also turned out to be a considerable burden. In October 2014, pharmaceutical company Gilead Sciences reported that the tax on prescription original drugs was $337 million, reducing earnings per share from $2.05 to $1.84 (Greenberg, 2015).

The increase in drug prices could have been influenced by several other factors, such as FDA regulations, pricing strategies, or the situation on other markets. However, drug manufacturers had to take some adjustment measures because the sale of drugs

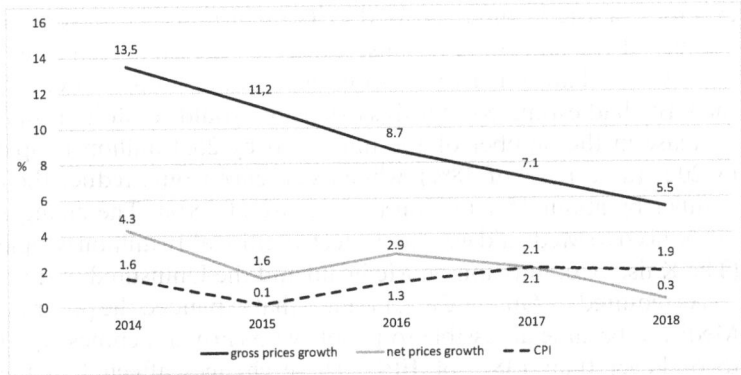

Figure 3.10 Dynamics of the increase in the prices of original drugs (in per cent) in the years 2014–2018

Note: Gross prices have been estimated based on wholesale transactions and do not consider the various discounts reducing the net revenues of the producers. Net prices include discounts granted and other forms of rebates.

Source: Own study, based on: IQVIA Institute, 2019.

below market prices to a growing number of the insured posed a risk of chronic losses or lower than expected profits. In this context, it is worth noting that, according to the data presented by the analytical company IQVIA, the increase in net prices of original drugs (i.e., after discounts, etc.) was much lower than the increase in gross prices. Furthermore, in the years 2012–2014 there was a situation when the dynamics of net price growth decreased (9.1%; 4.8%; 4.5%) and gross prices increased (10%; 11.4%; 13.7%) (IQVIA Institute, 2017). Although recent data indicate an increasingly slower increase in gross prices (a decrease in dynamics), these figures are still significantly higher than the increase in net prices and CPI (Figure 3.10). This should not be surprising because the lower increase in net prices is due to, for example, factors such as discounts or other benefits that the insured receive.

Other effects

Increase in the number of the insured in Medicaid

In the context of the consequences of the introduction of ObamaCare, public attention was directed to the marketplaces/

exchanges, mainly due to a significant increase in premiums, direct expenses of the insured, or loud exits of insurers. However, the number of the uninsured was also caused by the expansion of eligibility for Medicaid. Even before ObamaCare went into effect, the CBO had estimated that this extension would result in a total decrease in the number of the uninsured by 25.3 million people by 2022 (a decrease of 48%), while its absence would reduce their number by about 15.1 million (a decrease of 28%). The changes introduced to Medicaid were to protect additional 10 million people (The Kaiser Commission on Medicaid and the Uninsured, 2013).

As required by ObamaCare, in states that expanded the program Medicaid became accessible to people who earned incomes equal to or lower than 138% of FPL. These changes affected to the greatest extent adults (19–64 years old) with low incomes without health insurance. Therefore, in states that expanded Medicaid, the decline in the percentage of the uninsured among this group was more noticeable – between 2013 and 2017 it was -9.3% compared to -3.7% for states that had not chosen to expand Medicaid (Rudowitz & Antonisse, 2018).

In 2019, a total of 72.8 million people were enrolled in Medicaid (in 2013 it was 55.4 million insured, an increase of 31%). 14.8 million of them (20%) were adults who had insured themselves because of information about the extension of Medicaid. The largest part of this new group (12 million) consisted of people who enrolled in this insurance thanks to the extension of its eligibility by ObamaCare – these were the so-called newly eligible for Medicaid. In turn, the rest (2.8 million) had been eligible for Medicaid even before ObamaCare (not newly eligible for Medicaid), but for various reasons had not been previously insured (KFF, c).

What is significant, the number of people insured by Medicaid is higher from previous CBO estimates primarily because a significant number of people have not insured themselves through marketplaces/exchanges, and Medicaid is a cheaper alternative for some of them. Brian Blasé, a former Special Assistant to the President from 2017 to 2019, points out that the number of Medicaid insured is significantly higher than the CBO estimates from 2010 and from 2014 to 2015, when ObamaCare took effect. In states that expanded Medicaid, enrolment rates were about 50% higher than the CBO estimated, contributing to an increase in spending. In 2015, government spending on a new Medicaid insured was $6,366 compared to $4,281 and 4,200 forecast by CMS and CBO a year earlier (Blase, 2017).

Thus, the total spending on Medicaid expansion was also higher than expected. Back in 2014, the CBO estimated the cost of expanding Medicaid in 2015 would be $42 billion. However, these expenses ultimately amounted to $68 billion and were 68% higher than previously forecast. Blase concludes that the CBO did not adequately anticipate the response of states that set higher payment rates for insurers due to the expansion of Medicaid (Blasé, 2017). Some states introduced the private option, which allowed them to use Medicaid funds to purchase private health plans in state marketplaces/exchanges. The first state to receive approval to introduce such solutions was Arkansas (2014). In this state, a small proportion of the insured with worse health were qualified for traditional Medicaid, and the rest were assigned for the private option. The insured through the private option do not pay premiums, only people with incomes above 100% FPL incur small direct costs. However, they do not exceed the federal limit of 5% of household income (Maylone & Sommers, 2017).

This solution is one of the possible modifications to the state's Medicaid extension programs. Others include introduction of premiums, a higher share of direct beneficiaries' expenses, introduction of incentives for a healthy lifestyle, or restrictions on medical transport in non-emergency situations. Some states have used different combinations of them. For instance, Iowa and Michigan introduced Medicaid premiums, but added the opportunity for beneficiaries to lower them through various measures aiming at improving their health. Indiana, on the other hand, imposed fees for unpaid premiums and introduced the inability to re-enrol in Medicaid for six months. At the end of 2016, a total of eight states had approval to use the above modifications intended to give them more flexibility in developing their state Medicaid programs (Blase, 2017).

However, even before ObamaCare came into force, more than 4 million people had not been enrolled in this program despite meeting the criteria set. Some reasons for this attitude include access to medical services in emergency cases despite the lack of insurance, the desire to avoid the registration process, or simply the lack of such a need. Therefore, wider access to this program did not necessarily have to benefit everyone eligible for it. This is confirmed by the Kaiser Family Foundation, according to which out of 27.9 million uninsured adults in 2018, as many as 15.9 million (57%) were eligible for Medicaid or to receive financial support on marketplaces/exchanges. In turn, the remaining 12 million uninsured were not eligible to receive such support because of: earning too high income, the possibility of joining the insurance offered by the employer, their immigration status, and the so-called coverage gap occurring in states that had not expanded Medicaid (Figure 3.11).

The data in Figure 3.11 show that the mere possibility of receiving financial support is not everything. The largest group of uninsured adults are those who can receive tax credits (33%), but significant increases in premiums and other payments are one of the main barriers that effectively discourage them from doing

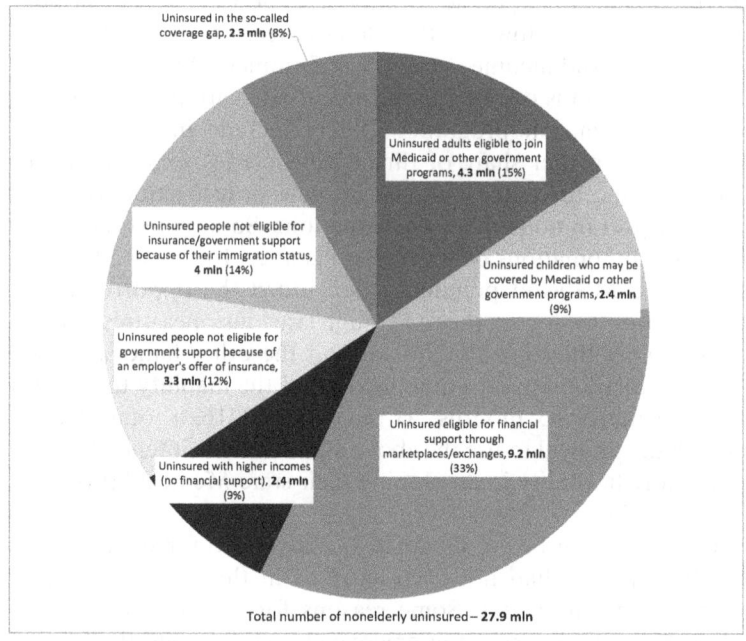

Figure 3.11 Eligibility of individual groups of uninsured adults to receive support under ObamaCare in 2018

Source: Own study, based on: J. Tolbert et al., 2019.

so. Also, at least part of the 24% eligible for Medicaid, CHIP, or some state programs, prefer to remain uninsured despite incurring minimal or no deductible expenses. A further 20% of the uninsured are people with higher incomes or insurance offered by the employer, so in their case the lack of insurance does not have to lead to serious financial and health consequences. In addition to the 14% of immigrants who cannot get government support due to legislation, out of the nearly 28 million uninsured about 8% of live in states that have not expanded Medicaid.

In turn, according to other studies conducted by researchers from, for example, the Massachusetts Institute of Technology and Harvard, it appears that the increase in the number of the insured, associated with receiving financial support under ObamaCare (in 2014–2015) was only in 40% the result of receiving reliefs and subsidies through marketplaces/exchanges. The remainder of this increase (60%) was accounted for by Medicaid, with about half (30%) being insured people who had been eligible for the program before ObamaCare and "only" 20% of newly eligible adults (Frean et al., 2017, p. 72). On this basis, it can be concluded that joining this insurance by people who had been able to do it before (at least partially) was related to the publicity associated with ObamaCare and with the Medicaid extension (the so-called *woodwork effect*).

Consequently, the structure of the uninsured is heterogeneous and that the lack of insurance should not be equated with an undesirable situation for the uninsured. Moreover, not all the 2.3 million uninsured in the coverage gap need to feel the need to enrol in government insurance. In more than a dozen states that have not expanded Medicaid, there is a lower level of FPL (40% on average) covering mainly parents with children and not childless people. The latter group, with income in the range of 40-100% FPL, does not have access to Medicaid and falls in the *gap*. However, if their income is at least 100% FPL, they can receive support through marketplaces/exchanges. In states where Medicaid was not expanded in 2018, an additional 2.1 million uninsured were people with incomes in the range of 100-138% FPL, and thus already eligible for financial support through marketplaces/exchanges, who for some reason did not join the insurance (Figure 3.12) (Garfield et al., 2020). There is also no guarantee that all of them will enrol in Medicaid even after its expansion. This leads to the clear and repeatedly mentioned conclusion that the possibility of insurance

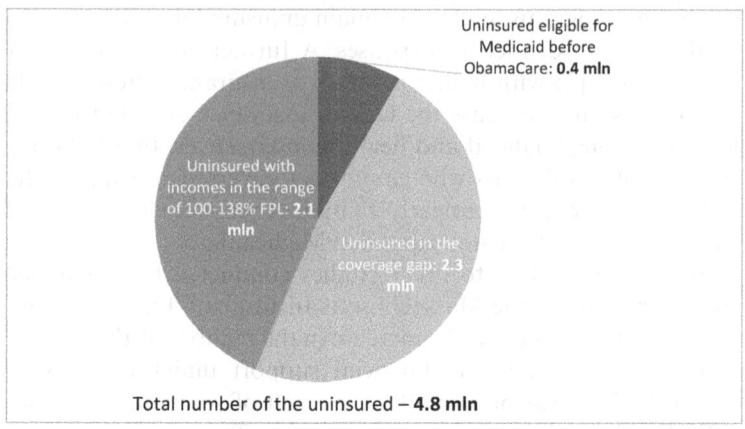

Figure 3.12 Number and structure of uninsured adults potentially bene-
fiting from Medicaid extension

Source: Own study, based on: R. Garfield et al., 2020.

does not have to be used by everyone who qualifies for it. There
can be many reasons for such an attitude. However, it should be
emphasized that from an economic point of view, the lack of
insurance does not mean a lack of access to medical services.

Therefore, it turns that expanding Medicaid beyond
marketplaces/exchanges leads to further marginalization of direct
spending and disrupts the rational financing structure of access
to health services. Several states (e.g., Arkansas), to improve the
rationalization of benefits, have introduced an additional employment requirement to access Medicaid (Collins & Bhupal, 2019).

Interestingly, as in the case of marketplaces/exchanges,
Medicaid also has a large turnover of the insured. According to
the Commonwealth Fund, of the 9 million people (25–63 years
old) enrolled in Medicaid in January 2014, only 66.7% remained
insured in December 2015. The remaining 33.3% (about 3 million)
were out of the program permanently or temporarily, of which
2.2 million (24.5%) did not receive any other type of insurance. One of the reasons for this situation is the administrative
barriers that require the submission of appropriate documentation
during the registration process or when re-joining the insurance.

Seasonal work is indicated as another reason. For instance, people employed in agriculture usually do not have insurance offered by their employer. During several months of work, their income may increase above a given threshold, which may result in the loss of Medicaid entitlements. In turn, after the end of seasonal work, their income decreases, which means that they again become eligible for Medicaid. In search of solutions to such problems, it is proposed, among other things, to abolish additional employment requirements or to expand Medicaid in states that have not yet done so (Collins & Glied, 2018). However, this leads to a situation in which Medicaid is increasingly beginning to resemble a single-payer system with increasing costs, expenses and less and less liability of the insured.

Other consequences

The expansion of Medicaid, like the granting tax credits in marketplaces/exchanges, leads to a weaker motivation to work and achieve higher incomes, and thus to greater financial independence. Higher incomes may result in a person previously qualified for Medicaid or to have part of their health insurance covered losing such status.

For example, a 60-year-old person with an annual income of $49,960 (2020) with a silver plan can count on covering 58% of their premiums with the tax credit granted – the monthly premium paid by the insured drops from $979 to $407. However, if the annual income of such a person increases by $10 to $49,970, then they lose the right to such support and already incur 100% of expenses (KFF, 2020). Although the change in the income is not noticeable, such provisions can effectively discourage from achieving gradual and long-term salary increases for fear of losing insurance or incurring higher expenses. It can be similar in the case of Medicaid expansion, where an increase in income above 138% of FPL already leads to ineligibility for this program.

There were also attempts to justify the expansion of Medicaid by the fact that it contributed to saving more lives. These arguments were particularly raised at a time when the Trump administration made efforts to repeal ObamaCare. However, as Oren Cass of the Manhattan Institute points out, attempts to demonstrate the positive impact of Medicaid expansion were based on extrapolation of previous studies focusing on private insurance. Other numerous studies involving Medicaid showed no improvement in the health of the insured.[10] Where such an effect occurred, it mainly involved pregnant women and children, that is, groups that had been covered by insurance even before ObamaCare (Cass, 2017).

According to the researcher, ObamaCare's positive impact on the health of the population should be supported by appropriate statistics. Meanwhile, in 2015, mortality (age-adjusted) increased, and life expectancy in the USA fell for the first time since the early 1990s. In 2015, 30,000 more deaths were recorded than if the mortality rate had remained at the level of 2014. This figure would amount to 80,000 more deaths if the decrease in the mortality rate from 2000 to 2013 were considered. However, if a positive effect of Medicaid expansion were to occur, the states that expanded the program should show slower increases (or decreases) in mortality compared to the states where such an expansion had not occurred. Meanwhile, in the first group there was a higher increase in mortality (by 9 deaths per 100,000 population), while in the second group it amounted to 6 deaths per 100,000 population. Cass points out that what may be behind these statistics are factors such as, for example, the increase in obesity or the opioid crisis, which may have had a lower intensity in the states that had not expanded Medicaid, and one should not draw too clear conclusions from this. It is important, however, that according to many studies, ObamaCare did not contribute to the decrease in mortality, thus, it should not be considered as an argument for maintaining it (Cass, 2017).

The last point to look out for is the financing of ObamaCare spending. John C. Goodman (2015) points out that about half of them have their origin in Medicare cuts, which leads to lower payments to suppliers in this program. Payments for hospital services in Medicare and Medicaid programs in 2012 amounted to 68% and 70% of payment rates in private insurance respectively (Cass, 2017). However, in 2018 they fell to about 58%. According to CMS forecasts, the decline in the rates of these payments will continue in the coming decades and in 2050 they are to amount to about 50% of the payments in private insurance, and in 2090 – 40%. These cuts are based on the so-called productivity adjustments which began in 2012, whose purpose was to shift funds from Medicare so that financial support for the insured in the marketplaces/exchanges through tax credits could be made.

In addition, upper payment limits (UPLs) were introduced for Medicaid, including for hospital or outpatient services. This means that the total Medicaid payments for services in these individual categories cannot exceed the amounts that would be paid for the same services in Medicare (except for payments for medical services) (Shatto & Clemens, 2020, pp. 4–5).

Similar cuts are taking place in the case of payments for medical services. In 2017, the level of payments for this type of service in Medicare was 75% of payment rates in private insurance, but in 2030 this share is expected to fall to about 60%, in 2060 to about 40%, and in 2094 it is to be only 26% and (at the same time) less than half the rates in Medicaid (Shatto & Clemens, 2020, pp. 5–6).

This clearly demonstrates that the ObamaCare goals are met at the expense of other beneficiaries of the government insurance, and that this reform does not really create any added value.

Notes

1 However, in this case it could be described as a spiral of (un) affordability.
2 The last year before ObamaCare.
3 In a given health plan, in addition to own contribution, it is also possible to make co-payments and co-insurance in parallel.
4 For instance, for an insured person with income in the range of 100–150% FPL in 2020, it is $2,700 (individual variant) and $5,400 (family variant). In turn, for a person with income in the range of 200–250% FPL it is $6,500 and $13,000, respectively.
5 In the states using the HealthCate.gov.
6 That is, their expenditure on deductible exceeds 5% (200% FPL<) or 10% of income.
7 Or not having the status of an inherited health plan.
8 For health plans whose policy year began on or before 1 October 2020.
9 The higher value of any of these options was decisive.
10 Such research was carried in, for example, Oregon.

References

Alltucker, K. (2016). Close call: How Pinal County could have been the only place in the USA with no 'Obamacare' choice, https://eu.azcentral.com/story/money/business/health/2016/09/08/blue-cross-agrees-to-sell-health-plans-through-obamacare-in-pinal-county/89981732/ (accessed: 26.08.2020).

Appleby, J., & Gorman, A. (2013). Thousands of consumers get insurance cancellation notices due to health law changes, https://khn.org/news/cancellation-notices-health-insurance/ (accessed: 01.09.2020).

Avery, K., Gardner, M., Gee, E., Marchetti-Bowick, E., McDowell, A., & Sen, A. (2015). Health plan choice and premiums in the 2016 Health Insurance Marketplace, https://aspe.hhs.gov/system/files/pdf/135461/2016%20Marketplace%20Premium%20Landscape%20Issue%20Brief%2010-30-15%20FINAL.pdf (accessed: 12.08.2020).

Bartz, D. (2017). US blocks health insurer Aetna's $34 billion Humana acquisition, www.reuters.com/article/us-humana-aetna-antitrust-idUSKBN1572BF (accessed: 25.08.2020).

Belk, D. (2016). The skyrocketing cost of brand name prescription drugs, www.huffpost.com/entry/the-skyrocketing-cost-of-_b_7492476?guccounter=1 (accessed: 09.09.2020).

Blasé, B. (2016). Obamacare's maze turned millions into lawbreakers, https://fee.org/articles/obamacares-maze-turned-millions-into-lawbreakers/ (accessed: 14.08.2020).

Blasé, B. (2017). Learning from CBO's history of incorrect ObamaCare projections, www.forbes.com/sites/theapothecary/2017/01/02/learning-from-cbos-history-of-incorrect-obamacare-projections/#2e2012ca46a7 (accessed: 24.09.2022).

Cannon, M. F. (2017). How ObamaCare punishes the sick, www.wsj.com/articles/how-obamacare-punishes-the-sick-1488327340 (accessed 13.08.2020).

Carpenter, E., & Sloan, C. (2018). Health plans with more restrictive provider networks continue to dominate the exchange market, https://avalere.com/press-releases/health-plans-with-more-restrictive-provider-networks-continue-to-dominate-the-exchange-market (accessed: 13.08.2020).

Cass, O. (2017). Will repealing Obamacare kill people?, https://media4.manhattan-institute.org/sites/default/files/IB-OC-0217.pdf (accessed: 28.09.2020).

Centers for Medicare & Medicaid Services (2016). Summary report in transitional reinsurance payments and permanent risk adjustment transfers for the 2015 benefit year, www.cms.gov/CCIIO/Programs-and-Initiatives/Premium-Stabilization-Programs/Downloads/June-30-2016-RA-and-RI-Summary-Report-5CR-063016.pdf (accessed: 24.08.2020).

Centers for Medicare & Medicaid Services (2017). Health Insurance Marketplaces 2017 open enrollment period. Final enrollment report: November 1, 2016 – January 31, 2017, www.cms.gov/newsroom/fact-sheets/health-insurance-marketplaces-2017-open-enrollment-period-final-enrollment-report-november-1-2016 (accessed: 19.08.2020).

Centers for Medicare & Medicaid Services (2018). Health Insurance Exchanges 2018 open enrollment period final report, www.cms.gov/newsroom/fact-sheets/health-insurance-exchanges-2018-open-enrollment-period-final-report#_ftn8 (accessed: 21.08.2020).

Centers for Medicare & Medicaid Services (2019a). Insurance Standards Bulletin Series – INFORMATION – Extension of limited non-enforcement policy through 2020, www.cms.gov/ CCIIO/Resources/Regulations-and-Guidance/Downloads/Limi ted-Non-Enforcement-Policy-Extension-Through-CY2020.pdf (accessed: 01.09. 2020).

Centers for Medicare & Medicaid Services (2019b). Plan Year 2020 qualified health plan choice and premiums in HealthCare.gov states, www. cms.gov/CCIIO/Resources/Data-Resources/Downloads/2020QHPP remiumsChoiceReport.pdf (accessed: 12.08.2020).

Centers for Medicare & Medicaid Services (2020). Health Insurance Exchanges 2020 open enrollment report, www.cms.gov/files/document/ 4120-health-insurance-exchanges-2020-open-enrollment-report-final. pdf (accessed 14.08.2020).

Centers for Medicare & Medicaid Services (n. d.). Final HHS notice of benefit and payment parameters for 2020 fact sheet, www.cms.gov/ CCIIO/Resources/Fact-Sheets-and-FAQs/Downloads/CMS-9926-F-Fact-Sheet.pdf (accessed: 18.08.2020).

Cigna (2019). Three ACA taxes repealed and 5th Circuit decision in two major events this week, www.cigna.com/employers-brokers/insights/ informed-on-reform/news/three-aca-taxes-repealed-and-fifth-circuit-decision-this-week (accessed: 02.09.2020).

Cigna (n. d.). Cadillac tax, www.cigna.com/employers-brokers/insights/ informed-on-reform/cadillac-tax (accessed: 02.09.2020).

Clemans-Cope, L., & Anderson, N. (2015). QuickTake: Health insurance policy cancellations were uncommon in 2014, http://hrms.urban.org/ quicktakes/Health-Insurance-Policy-Cancellations-Were-Uncommon-in-2014.html (accessed: 01.09.2020).

Collins, S. R., Bhupal, H. K., & Doty, M. M. (2019). Health insurance coverage eight years after the ACA, www.commonwealthfund.org/ publications/issue-briefs/2019/feb/health-insurance-coverage-eight-years-after-aca (accessed: 25.09.2020).

Collins, S. R., Glied, S. A., & Jackson, A. (2018). The potential implications of work requirements for the insurance coverage of Medicaid beneficiaries: The case of Kentucky, www.commonwealthf und.org/publications/2018/oct/kentucky-medicaid-work-requirements (accessed: 25.09.2020).

Commonwealth Fund (2017). Essential facts about health reform alternatives: Eliminating cost-sharing reductions, www.commo nwealthfund.org/publications/explainer/2017/apr/essential-facts-about-health-reform-alternatives-eliminating-cost?redirect_source= /publications/explainers/2017/apr/cost-sharing-reductions (accessed: 18.08.2020).

Cox, C., Long, M., Semanskee, A., Kamal, R., Claxton, G., & Levitt, L. (2016a). 2017 premium changes and insurer participation in the

Affordable Care Act's Health Insurance Marketplaces, www.kff.org/health-reform/issue-brief/2017-premium-changes-and-insurer-partic ipation-in-the-affordable-care-acts-health-insurance-marketplaces/ (accessed: 13.08.2020).

Cox, C., Semanskee, A., Claxton, G., & Levitt, L. (2016b). Explaining health care reform: Risk adjustment, reinsurance, and risk corridors, www.kff.org/health-reform/issue-brief/explaining-health-care-reform-risk-adjustment-reinsurance-and-risk-corridors/ (accessed: 24.08.2020).

Daemmrich, A. (2011). *US Healthcare reform and the pharmaceutical industry*. Harvard Business School.

Department of Health and Human Services (2017). Trump administration takes action to abide by the law and constitution, discontinue CSR payments, www.hhs.gov/about/news/2017/10/12/trump-administration-takes-action-abide-law-constitution-discontinue-csr-payments.html (accessed: 18.08.2020).

Donohue, J. M., & Huskamp, H. A. (2018). 'Doughnuts and discounts – Changes to Medicare Part D under the Bipartisan Budget Act of 2018', *The New England Journal of Medicine, 21*: 1957–1960.

Drug Discovery Trends Editor (2015). US pharmaceutical market value will approach $550 billion by 2020: GlobalData, www.drugdiscoverytre nds.com/u-s-pharmaceutical-market-value-will-approach-550-billion-by-2020-globaldata/ (accessed: 08.09.2020).

Fehr, R., Cox, C., & Levitt, L. (2018). Insurer participation on ACA marketplaces, 2014–2019, http://files.kff.org/attachment/Issue-Brief-Insurer-Participation-on-ACA-Marketplaces-2014-2019 (accessed: 26.08.2020).

Fehr, R., Kamal, R., & Cox, C. (2019). Insurer participation on ACA marketplaces, 2014–2020, www.kff.org/private-insurance/issue-brief/insurer-participation-on-aca-marketplaces-2014-2020/?fbclid= IwAR2vYZrcKrmvln594bOVZD4gfiGfBXA-W4sdA-WLKOFQeIIp L_OBrSqfMIs (accessed: 26.08.2020).

Fox, B., & Brod, M. (2019). Underinsured rate rose from 2014–2018. With greatest growth among people in employer health plans, www. commonwealthfund.org/press-release/2019/underinsured-rate-rose-2014-2018-greatest-growth-among-people-employer-health (accessed: 18.08.2020).

Frean, M., Gruber, J., & Sommers, B. D. (2017). 'Premium subsidies, the mandate, and Medicaid expansion: Coverage effects of the Affordable Care Act', *Journal of Health Economics, 53*: 72–86.

FRED (n. d. a). Consumer Price Index for all urban consumers: All items in US city average (CPIAUCSL), https://fred.stlouisfed.org/series/CPIAUCSL#0 (accessed: 12.08.2020).

FRED (n. d. b). Consumer Price Index for all urban consumers: Medical care in US city average (CPIMEDSL), https://fred.stlouisfed.org/series/CPIMEDSL#0 (accessed: 12.08.2020).

French, H. E., & Smith, M. P. (2015). 'Anatomy of a slow-motion health insurance death spiral', *North American Actuarial Journal, 1*: 60–72.

Galewitz, P. (2016). Seven remaining Obamacare co-ops prepare survival strategies, https://khn.org/news/seven-remaining-obamacare-co-ops-prepare-survival-strategies/ (accessed: 25.08.2020).

Garfield, R., Orgera, K., & Damico, A. (2020). The coverage gap: Uninsured poor adults in States that do not expand Medicaid, www.kff.org/medicaid/issue-brief/the-coverage-gap-uninsured-poor-adults-in-states-that-do-not-expand-medicaid/ (accessed: 25.09.2020).

Geruso, M., Layton, T., & Prinz, D. (2019). 'Screening in contract design: Evidence from the ACA Health Insurance Exchanges', *American Economic Journal: Economic Policy, 2*: 64–107.

Goodman, J. C. (2015). Six problems with the ACA that aren't going away, www.healthaffairs.org/do/10.1377/hblog20150625.048781/full/ (accessed: 29.09.2020).

Goodman, J. C., Musgrave, G. L., & Herrick, D. M. (2004). *Lives at risk. Single-payer national health insurance around the world.* Rowman & Littlefield Publishers.

Goodnough, A., Abelson, R., Sanger-Katz, M., & Kliff, S. (2020). ObamaCare turns 10. Here's a look at what works and doesn't, www.nytimes.com/2020/03/23/health/obamacare-aca-coverage-cost-history.html (accessed: 18.08.2020).

Greenberg, S. (2015). Five years later: ACA's branded prescription drug fee may have contributed to rising drug prices, https://taxfoundation.org/five-years-later-aca-s-branded-prescription-drug-fee-may-have-contributed-rising-drug-prices/ (accessed: 09.09.2020).

Harvard Business School (2016). The failed launch of www.HealthCare.gov, https://digital.hbs.edu/platform-rctom/submission/the-failed-launch-of-www-healthcare-gov/# (accessed: 20.08.2020).

Hawkins, C. C., & Hwang, A. (2018). Cutting employee hours to avoid ACA requirements costs employer $7.4 Million, www.dwt.com/blogs/employment-labor-and-benefits/2018/12/cutting-employee-hours-to-avoid-aca-requirements-c (accessed: 03.09.2020).

HealthCare.gov (n. d.). Out-of-pocket maximum/limit, www.healthcare.gov/glossary/out-of-pocket-maximum-limit/ (accessed: 17.08.2020).

Henderson, D. R. (2016). Even left-leaning econ writers are impoverished by Obamacare, https://fee.org/articles/even-left-leaning-econ-writers-are-impoverished-by-obamacare/ (accessed: 02.09.2020).

Hyman, D. A., & Silver, C. (2018). *Overcharged: Why Americans pay too much for health care.* Cato Institute.

Internal Revenue Service (n. d. a). Annual fee on branded prescription drug manufacturers and importers, www.irs.gov/affordable-care-act/annual-fee-on-branded-prescription-drug-manufacturers-and-import ers (accessed: 09.09.2020).

Internal Revenue Service (n. d. b). Information reporting by applicable large employers, www.irs.gov/affordable-care-act/employers/informat ion-reporting-by-applicable-large-employers (accessed: 02.09.2020).

Internal Revenue Service (n. d. c). Premium Tax Credit: Claiming the credit and reconciling advance credit payments, www.irs.gov/affordable-care-act/individuals-and-families/premium-tax-credit-claiming-the-cre dit-and-reconciling-advance-credit-payments (accessed: 14.08.2020).

IQVIA Institute (2017). Medicines use and spending in the US: A review of 2016 and outlook to 2021 Institute Report, www.iqvia.com/insights/the-iqvia-institute/reports/medicines-use-and-spending-in-the-us-a-rev iew-of-2016 (accessed: 09.09.2020).

IQVIA Institute (2019). Medicine use and spending in the US: A review of 2018 and outlook to 2023, https://static1.squarespace.com/static/54d50ceee4b05797b34869cf/t/5cd765e5c49ce70001f3449a/1557620199 759/medicine-use-and-spending-in-the-us---a-review-of-2018-outlook-to-2023.pdf (accessed: 09.09.2020).

Japsen, B. (2013). Obamacare will bring drug industry $35 billion in profits, www.forbes.com/sites/brucejapsen/2013/05/25/obamacare-will-bring-drug-industry-35-billion-in-profits/#13eddbd534a5 (accessed: 08.09.2020).

Japsen, B. (2017). Humana to fully exit Obamacare in 2018, www.for bes.com/sites/brucejapsen/2017/02/14/humana-will-leave-obamac are-in-2018-citing-unstable-risk-pools/#441a960370c1 (accessed: 25.08.2020).

The Kaiser Commission on Medicaid and the Uninsured (2013). *Medicaid: A primer. Key information on the nation's health coverage program for low-income people.* Kaiser Family Foundation.

Kamal, R., Cox, C., Shoaibi, C., Kaplun, B., Semanskee, A., & Levitt, L. (2017). An early look at 2018 premium changes and insurer participation on ACA exchanges, www.kff.org/health-reform/issue-brief/an-early-look-at-2018-premium-changes-and-insurer-participation-on-aca-exchanges/ (accessed: 13.08.2020).

Keith, K. (2019). Latest ruling over unpaid CSRs, www.healthaffairs.org/do/10.1377/hblog20191025.570658/full/ (accessed: 18.08.2020).

Keith, K. (2020). Supreme Court rules that insurers are entitled to risk corridors payments: What the court said and what happens next, www.healthaffairs.org/do/10.1377/hblog20200427.34146/full/ (accessed: 24.08.2020).

KFF (Kaiser Family Foundation) (2017). Estimates: Average ACA Marketplace premiums for silver plans would need to increase by 19%

to compensate for lack of funding for cost-sharing subsidies, www.kff. org/health-reform/press-release/estimates-average-aca-marketplace-premi ums-for-silver-plans-would-need-to-increase-by-19-to-compensate-for-lack-of-funding-for-cost-sharing-subsidies/?utm_campaign=KFF-2017-April-Eliminating-ACA-Cost-Sharing-Payments&utm_content=54538 233&utm_medium=social&utm_source=facebook (accessed: 18.08.2020).

KFF (Kaiser Family Foundation) (2019a). Analysis: 'Cadillac Tax' on high-cost health plans could affect 1 in 5 employers in 2022, www. kff.org/private-insurance/press-release/analysis-cadillac-tax-on-high-cost-health-plans-could-affect-1-in-5-employers-in-2022/ (accessed: 02.09.2020).

KFF (Kaiser Family Foundation) (2019b). Cost-sharing for plans offered in the federal marketplace, 2014–2020, www.kff.org/slideshow/cost-shar ing-for-plans-offered-in-the-federal-marketplace-2014-2020/ (accessed: 17.08.2020).

KFF (Kaiser Family Foundation) (2019c). *Employer health benefits 2019 annual survey*. Kaiser Family Foundation.

KFF (Kaiser Family Foundation) (2019d). Medicare Part D beneficiaries who reach the catastrophic coverage limit can expect to pay more out-of-pocket for their prescription drugs next year, www.kff.org/medicare/ press-release/medicare-part-d-beneficiaries-who-reach-the-catastrop hic-coverage-limit-can-expect-to-pay-more-out-of-pocket-for-their-prescription-drugs-next-year/ (accessed: 08.09.2020).

KFF (Kaiser Family Foundation) (2020). Health Insurance Marketplace calculator, www.kff.org/interactive/subsidy-calculator/#state=&zip= &income-type=dollars&income=49960&employer-coverage= 0&people=1&alternate-plan-family=&adult-count=1&adu lts%5B0%5D%5Bage%5D=50&adults%5B0%5D%5Btobacco%5D= 0&child-count=0 (accessed: 26.09.2020).

KFF (Kaiser Family Foundation) (n. d. a). Marketplace average bench-mark premiums, www.kff.org/health-reform/state-indicator/marketpl ace-average-benchmark-premiums/?currentTimeframe=0&selectedDi stributions=2014--2020&sortModel=%7B%22colId%22:%22Locat ion%22,%22sort%22:%22asc%22%7D (accessed: 12.08.2020).

KFF (Kaiser Family Foundation) (n. d. b). Marketplace average premiums and average Advanced Premium Tax Credit (APTC), www. kff.org/health-reform/state-indicator/marketplace-average-premi ums-and-average-advanced-premium-tax-credit-aptc/?currentTimefr ame=3&sortModel=%7B%22colId%22:%22Location%22,%22s ort%22:%22asc%22%7D (accessed: 13.08.2020).

KFF (Kaiser Family Foundation) (n. d. c). Medicaid expansion enroll-ment, www.kff.org/health-reform/state-indicator/medicaid-expansion-enr ollment/?currentTimeframe=0&sortModel=%7B%22colId%22:%22L ocation%22,%22sort%22:%22asc%22%7D (accessed: 24.09.2022).

Kodjak, A. (2016). UnitedHealth to leave most Obamacare exchanges in 2017, www.npr.org/sections/health-shots/2016/04/19/474834930/unite dhealth-to-leave-most-obamacare-exchanges-in-2017?t=1598333130 368 (accessed: 25.08.2020).

Laszewski, R. (2015). Why are the 2016 Obamacare rate increases so large?, www.forbes.com/sites/realspin/2015/06/10/why-are-the-2016-obamac are-rate-increases-so-large/#304f74a5103e (accessed: 13.08.2020).

Levinson D. R./Department of Health and Human Services – Office of the Inspector General (2015). Actual enrollment and profitability was lower than projections made by the consumer operated and oriented plans and might affect their ability to repay loans provided under the Affordable Care Act, https://oig.hhs.gov/oas/reports/region5/51400055. pdf (accessed: 25.08.2020).

Manhattan Institute (n. d. a). The Obamacare impact, https://media4. manhattan-institute.org/sites/default/files/knowyourrates/index.htm# (accessed: 12.08.2020).

Manhattan Institute (n. d. b). Obamacare map, www.manhattan-institute. org/knowyourrates (accessed: 12.08.2020).

Mathews, A. M., & Weaver, C. (2014). Sick drawn to new coverage: High rates of serious conditions in health law plans put pressure on premiums, www.wsj.com/articles/sick-drawn-to-new-coverage-in-hea lth-law-plans-1403656445 (accessed: 12.08. 2020).

Maurer, M. (2019). Finance chiefs relieved after repeal of Cadillac Tax, www.wsj.com/articles/finance-chiefs-relieved-after-repeal-of-cadillac-tax-11577137387 (accessed: 02.09.2020).

Maylone, B., & Sommers, B. D. (2017). Evidence from the private option: The Arkansas experience, www.commonwealthfund.org/publications/ issue-briefs/2017/feb/evidence-private-option-arkansas-experience (accessed: 24.09.2022).

McGuff, D., & Murphy, R. P. (2015). *The primal prescription: Surviving The 'sick care' sinkhole.* Primal Blueprint Publishing.

McKeown, T. (2013). „Dobrowolne ubezpieczenia zdrowotne. Czynniki wspierające rozwój i bariery. Prywatne ubezpieczenia zdrowotne jako element systemu opieki zdrowotnej w Irlandii [Voluntary private health insurance market in Ireland: Public-private mix]", *Wiadomości ubezpieczeniowe. Dodatkowe ubezpieczenia zdrowotne. Efektywny system na tle doświadczeń europejskich* [Insurance news. Additional health insurance. An effective system against the background of European experience], *4*: 81–85.

Medicare Interactive (n. d.). Phases of Part D coverage, www.medicare interactive.org/get-answers/medicare-prescription-drug-coverage-part-d/medicare-part-d-costs/phases-of-part-d-coverage   (accessed: September 08.09.2020).

Norris, L. (2020a). CO-OP health plans: Patients' interests first, www.heal thinsurance.org/obamacare/co-op-health-plans-put-patients-interests-first/ (accessed: 25.08.2020).

Norris, L. (2020b). Is there still a penalty for being uninsured?, www.heal thinsurance.org/obamacare-enrollment-guide/what-is-the-obamacare-penalty/ (accessed: 20.08.2020).

O'Neill Hayes, T. (2018). Understanding the policies that influence the cost of drugs, www.americanactionforum.org/insight/understanding-the-policies-that-influence-the-cost-of-drugs/ (accessed: 09.09.2020).

Pipes, S. C. (2016). Obamacare's co-op disaster: Only 7 remain, www.forbes.com/sites/sallypipes/2016/07/25/obamacares-co-op-disaster-an-unfunny-comedy-of-errors/#5c8295805d5b (accessed: August 25.08.2020).

Rudowitz, R., & Antonisse, L. (2018). Implications of the ACA Medicaid expansion: A look at the data and evidence, www.kff.org/medicaid/issue-brief/implications-of-the-aca-medicaid-expansion-a-look-at-the-data-and-evidence/ (accessed: 24.09.2022).

Shatto, J. D., & Clemens, M. K. (2020). *Projected Medicare expenditures under an illustrative scenario with alternative payment updates to Medicare providers*. Centers for Medicare & Medicaid Services.

Sheen, R. (2020). Dave & Buster's demonstrates importance of complying with the ACA, https://acatimes.com/dave-busters-demonstrates-imp ortance-of-complying-with-the-aca/ (accessed: 03.09.2020).

Simmons-Duffin, S. (2019). Trump is trying hard to thwart Obamacare. How's that going?, www.npr.org/sections/health-shots/2019/10/14/768731628/trump-is-trying-hard-to-thwart-obamacare-hows-that-going?t=1597901071409 (accessed: 20.08.2020).

Tolbert, J., Orgera, K., Singer, N., & Damico, A. (2019). Key facts about the uninsured population, https://files.kff.org/attachment//fact-sheet-key-facts-about-the-uninsured-population (accessed: 25.09.2020).

Tracer, Z. (2016). Aetna to quit most ACA markets, joining major insurers, www.benefitnews.com/news/aetna-to-quit-most-aca-markets-joining-major-insurers (accessed: 25.08.2020).

US Department of Justice (2017). US District Court blocks Aetna's acquisition of Humana, www.justice.gov/opa/pr/us-district-court-blo cks-aetna-s-acquisition-humana (accessed: 25.08.2020).

Whitehouse.gov (2017). CBO's failed Obamacare enrollment projections, www.whitehouse.gov/articles/cbos-failed-obamacare-enrollment-proj ections/ (accessed: 19.08.2020).

4 Overview and evaluation of proposals for modification of the solutions introduced by ObamaCare

Reasons for the necessity of further changes

It can be said that proposals or announcements of further changes result from the unreliability of the interventions applied. Increase in the amount of premiums and direct expenses incurred by the insured, loud cases of insurers exiting the marketplaces/exchanges, numerous cancellations of pre-existing plans, new obligations for employers, new taxes, limited supplier networks, and so on – all these factors directly or indirectly contributed to the proposal for further amendments in the existing law.

Currently, there are two general directions of change – one proposed by the Republicans and the other by the Democrats. The Republicans' actions assume at least partially weakening ObamaCare, for example, in the form of withdrawing support for insurers, cancelling part of taxes, or reducing the penalty for lack of insurance to zero. In turn, the Democrats, bearing in mind the above-mentioned problems, propose, for example, to extend the scope of government financial support reducing the amount of direct expenses incurred by the insured on marketplaces/exchanges, or to introduce a public option as an alternative to insurance concluded by the employer. However, neither of these options perceive pure-market solutions as those that can give a better effect than further interventions.

Furthermore, any changes must occur in a specific legal and institutional order, which affects their content or scope at least partially. For instance, Prof. Galles of Pepperdine University points out that the penalty for not having insurance had to be treated as a tax that Congress could legitimately impose. Otherwise, it would be interpreted as a regulation requiring Americans to have

DOI: 10.4324/9781003385158-5

compulsory health insurance, which would be unconstitutional. Therefore, on this basis (in 2012) the Supreme Court could also rule by a majority (5-4) on the constitutionality of ObamaCare (Galles, 2018).

In the case of ObamaCare, it was also important that spending on subsidies for the insured with lower income was not approved by Congress, which is one of the requirements before the creation of a new item in government spending. However, this was a deliberate move by President Obama who instructed the Department of Health and Human Services and the Treasury Department to raise adequate funds that would come from cuts in other programs. Importantly, which programs were to be covered by the cuts was never specified due to the possible resistance in Congress and among their beneficiaries (e.g., Medicare). As a result, from a political point of view, the subsidies received by the new insured by the marketplaces/exchanges were difficult to withdraw even in the absence of the adoption of new spending in Congress and if the Supreme Court decided that ObamaCare was unconstitutional. The fear of taking away the beneficiaries' subsidies (even despite their non-compliance with the Constitution) would meet with their dissatisfaction and criticism of the actions of Congress. The lack of specification of the sources of funds for new expenditure was, therefore, aimed at redirecting them to new beneficiaries as soon as possible and hindering future changes in their withdrawal (Galles, 2018).

This deliberate bending of regulations, although politically effective, can hardly be considered as open and fluid actions adhering to the established legal and institutional framework. In this case, the Republicans had to consider that their efforts to abolish ObamaCare altogether would lead to millions of insured people losing subsidies and, thus, incline them to consider other solutions.

US history also shows that the more decisive proposals for change were closely related to the election campaigns leading up to the presidential election. Media publicity and debates between the candidates allowed the proposed changes to be presented to virtually every American.

For instance, Prof. Custer (Georgia State University) points out that a recession in the early 1990s resulted in about 2 million Americans losing their jobs and their health insurance. This fact was used to propose changes to US health system during the 1992 presidential campaign by both candidates for the US presidency, George H. W. Bush and Bill Clinton. Interestingly, both proposals had many features in common with ObamaCare, such as the creation of special groups of insurance purchases like marketplaces/exchanges, the obligation to accept everyone willing to buy insurance, the requirement to have insurance, or subsidies for low-income families. Custer argues that these similarities are not coincidental and result from the government's limited ability to create such insurance markets (Custer, 2016). In other words, if the government wants to create affordable insurance for people out of work, or with lower incomes, it must resort to subsidies, taxes, or greater control by insurers. This also leads to the simple conclusion that the ObamaCare assumptions were not really any novelty in this area of economic policy.

The issue of changes in the health system is a topic that may affect the outcome of the presidential election. This was the case, for example, during the 2016 campaign. Jeffrey Tucker from the American Institute for Economic Research draws attention to the fact that for many Americans, President Obama's flagship project had already become notorious after two years from its entry into force. In turn, in 2016, which was an election year, Americans experienced a significant increase in their insurance premiums or an increase in direct spending. In the same year, there were also loud exits of insurers from the marketplaces/exchanges or even further bankruptcies of smaller entities (cooperatives). Moreover, a week before the election, it was announced that the increase in premiums for the next year would be from 25% to 90%, which was often raised by Trump during his speeches or advertisements with his participation. Hillary Clinton, on the other hand, focused on defending ObamaCare, and in interviews given before the campaign she identified this bill with HillaryCare, her own project of changes in health system from the first half of the 1990s. For some undecided voters, this may have given the impression that the Democratic candidate was not aware of the existing problems, which contrasted sharply with Trump's clear message pointing to the existing problems and announcing the repeal of ObamaCare (Tucker, 2016).

Health care was also a major topic during the 2020 presidential campaign. Trump, who was running for re-election, continued his narrative of abolishing or further weakening ObamaCare, for example, by withdrawing federal funds dedicated for Medicaid expansion or proposing to reduce subsidies to premiums. In turn, his Democratic opponent, Joe Biden, proposed further expansion of ObamaCare by increasing financial support for the insured in marketplaces/exchanges, or creating public options (like Medicare) that would be available to anyone and automatically include low-income people in states where Medicaid had not been expanded. Biden also proposed lowering age entitling to use the Medicare from 65 to 60 (Levitt, 2020).

The changes would also cover prescription drugs in the Medicare program. Trump pointed to the problem of high drug prices, and potential solutions would be to lower the prices of some drugs to their levels in other countries where prices are set by the government (e.g., in Germany or France) (Glassman, 2020), or to allow patients to import medicines from abroad. Biden, on the other hand, called for the federal government to be given the power to negotiate drug prices for Medicare and other public or private buyers. Drug prices would be limited to levels paid by other developed countries. Other changes would consist in further limiting the purchase of medicines from the insured people's own pockets and allowing them to import them from abroad (Levitt, 2020).

Therefore, these proposals are to some extent similar (e.g., import of medicines), but they also inappropriately perceive subsequent price controls as an effective means in the fight with high drug prices that could lead, for example, to lower investment in research into new drugs in the future. None of the candidates proposed more decisive actions aimed at, for example, limiting the FDA's influence on the drug approval process, or reducing the role of the third-party payer.

American Health Care Act (AHCA)

Attempts to repeal ObamaCare and create its alternative

The year 2017 was mainly marked by the Republicans' efforts to repeal and replace ObamaCare, which was especially evident during the work of the Senate. However, as has already been mentioned, the Republicans knew that about 20 million Americans had become new beneficiaries of the changes (marketplaces/exchanges and the expansion of Medicaid) and taking away their recently obtained privileges could cause them great dissatisfaction. For this reason, the subsequent proposals for changes discussed retaining many elements of ObamaCare and did not allow for the introduction of a real market alternative, for example, by deregulating the health insurance market or abolishing supply-side regulations (doctors, hospitals, etc.). The Republicans' attitude results also from the fact that, according to them, the government can provide access to affordable health care for at least part of the population. The difference between them and the Democrats is, therefore, the choice of interventionist measures to be taken to achieve this goal.

The changes proposed by the Republicans reached their most advanced form as the so-called American Health Care Act of 2017 (AHCA). The scope of changes, even after the May modifications, was quite wide. Among other things, 15 different taxes introduced by ObamaCare were to be withdrawn, including: taxes/penalties for not having insurance or failure to meet certain requirements by employers. Taxes on prescription drugs, health insurers, sales tax on medical devices, and many others were also to be abolished. The scope of the changes also assumed the withdrawal (by 2020) of tax credits and the program to reduce direct expenses for the insured on the marketplaces/exchanges. Moreover, the federal government, starting in 2020, was no longer to pay an increased premium for the new Medicaid insured in states that had expanded the program before March 2017. States could continue to insure people with incomes up to 138% FPL, but at the standard (lower) premium in the given state. The increased premium (90% in 2020) was to apply only to people enrolled before 2020 who did not have a break in insurance (The United States Senate Republican Policy Committee, 2017).

The AHCA Act also assumed introducing (from 2020) a new refundable tax credit which could cover people who did not have government insurance or insurance offered by the employer. This relief was to increase with age and its maximum limit per family was set at $14,000. In addition to the new relief, the allowable annual limit for deposits to medical savings accounts was also to increase significantly, which was to help finance routine medical services out of one's own pocket and not through insurance (The United States Senate Republican Policy Committee, 2017).

Another important goal of the AHCA was to stabilize the individual insurance market (and small groups of the insured) by creating a new federal Patient and State Stability Fund providing states with about $100 billion to stabilize marketplaces/exchanges between 2018 and 2026. These funds were to be devoted mainly to creating a pool of high-risk people with worse health. This was to relieve the young and healthier insured so that they would pay lower premiums. However, the markets would not be properly deregulated, as insurers would still be obliged to insure all the willing customers (guaranteed issue) and would have limited possibilities to differentiate premiums, for example, in relation to gender (community rating). In addition, the Patient and State Stability Fund planned to establish a Federal Invisible Risk Sharing Program to provide further financial support to insurers related to providing the insured with finances to access to medical services (The United States Senate Republican Policy Committee, 2017).

The Republicans, by creating high-risk pools supported by federal funds, wanted to preserve the privileges of people with higher health risks while relieving those remaining in the marketplaces/exchanges. However, the government's intervention was preserved by taking only a slightly altered form and hiding the increase in premiums by transferring the costs to taxpayers.

The introduction of these changes required support in Congress, and especially in the Senate, where several further modifications of the AHCA were developed. Despite this, none of them managed to get a majority of votes. The last attempt to repeal ObamaCare at least partially failed in late July 2017, when three Republican senators also voted against another proposed change under the name the Health Care Freedom Act (HCFA) (the vote was 49–51) (McAuliff, 2017).

Interestingly, the HCFA itself already contained a smaller range of changes compared to the AHCA,[1] mainly due to the desire to reach a consensus and introduce at least partial modifications. These further assumed the abolition of the obligation to have insurance and the requirements for employers. The state authorities were also to be given the opportunity to waive the requirements for providing adequate coverage of insurance (essential health benefits). In turn, tax credits and a program of reducing direct expenses that had so far been received by the insured on marketplaces/exchanges were to be preserved. Thus, the idea of creating state high-risk pools was abandoned. Insurers were still obliged to accept all applicants and apply certain rules when determining the premiums. Plans to cut funding for Medicaid expansion were also withdrawn (KFF (Kaiser Family Foundation), 2017).

Despite all these concessions to the original version, the Republicans still failed to achieve sufficient support in the Senate. Instead, another Tax Cuts and Jobs Act was passed, reducing the penalty for lack of health insurance to zero.

Causes of Republican failures

Undoubtedly, one of the problems behind the great difficulties with the repeal of ObamaCare was that some Republican politicians themselves supported some elements of the Bill, as did some of their constituents who were beneficiaries of the changes. Therefore, it was a fact that could not be ignored when designing subsequent modifications.

Careful observers also pointed out that the Republicans ultimately failed to come up with common and unified solutions as a viable alternative to ObamaCare. At the same time, it was inconsistent with the strategy adopted many years before aimed at repealing and replacing ObamaCare. While the first goal was easier to achieve and focused on criticizing the Democrats' plan, the second goal required greater commitment, including convincing their constituents of the legitimacy of the changes. Meanwhile, the Republican Party was mainly focused on achieving this first goal for the next few years. This led to a situation in which the Republicans, when they obtained a majority in Congress and when their candidate won the presidential election, still did not have a clear plan of change. Moreover, the work on its creation (including arrangements for tax repeal, limiting federal spending on Medicaid expansion, or withdrawing support for the insured) began to reveal divisions and conflicts within their party, which made the process even more difficult (Scott & Kliff, 2017).

Goodman points out that the difficulties in developing a common position also result from the history of this party. In previous decades, the Republicans had been mostly focused on at least partially repealing the laws previously introduced by the Democrats rather than creating new laws. Therefore, in a situation that required them to develop their own solutions, they could not rely on their own experiences from the past. Moreover, the Democrats understood well that to make significant changes, in addition to gaining more votes in Congress, the support of the media, special interest groups, think-tanks and other institutions was also needed. This was necessary to gain the favour of public opinion (Goodman, 2018).

Goodman also points out that a good opportunity to get support for repealing ObamaCare may have been the hearings held by congressional committees with the insured who had difficulty accessing the benefits guaranteed by ObamaCare. Such people could be easily identified, for example, through numerous media reports about Americans incurring significant out-of-pocket expenses on medicines and tests or having to travel long distances to be able to make a doctor's appointment from their own network. These cases pointed clearly to the structural flaws of ObamaCare that the Pro-Democratic media (e.g., the *New York Times*) stopped covering for fear they could indeed become an effective tool in the fight to repeal ObamaCare. However, the Republicans did not use these true and numerous stories to influence public opinion through the creation of these commissions or using various institutions. This passive attitude may also have given the partial impression that Republicans did not care so much about solving the problem, as their political opponents often reproached them (Goodman, 2018).

One of the main problems was the recently obtained privileges of the new insured people. This part of society, despite various problems of ObamaCare, became the beneficiaries of the changes and began to fear their loss. This impacted the Republicans who sought to secure their interests. Such actions, however, did not give a chance to repeal ObamaCare and caused internal divisions. Thus, a complete reversal of the introduced changes was unrealistic from a political point of view.

From an economic perspective, this phenomenon has been thoroughly described by Tullock as the so-called *transitional gains trap*. Tullock pointed out that many government programs designed to help a particular social group or industry ultimately fail. According to him, the cause of these failures is the loss of initial profits generated by these groups of beneficiaries, which over time begin to decrease until the moment when a given group no longer benefits from a given program. However, this group will continue to strive (e.g., by exerting political pressure) to maintain this programme, as its withdrawal would mean the loss of its influence, and so on.[2]

This can be illustrated by the privileges that American citrus producers obtained in the 1930s during the Great Depression. They made it possible to control their production and to create a cartel limiting the quantity of citrus fruit put on the market, which naturally led to an increase in their prices. Thanks to the privileges obtained, no one was afraid of the consequences of breaking the antitrust law. Another consequence of these actions was an increase in the value of the land belonging to the cartel members caused by higher revenues from the sale of fruit. Subsequent people willing to purchase this land (and privileges) had to pay an increasingly higher price, the increase of which, however, meant that subsequent owners did not derive any extraordinary profits from its possession. In this case, the group that benefited most from the cartel was the original owners of the land at the time of its creation. Although subsequent owners no longer make any special profits, they will still strive to preserve their privileges. Their abolition would mean that they would suffer large losses because of the falling prices. Previously, this group had incurred significant expenditures on the purchase of land, but without the possibility of achieving extraordinary profits. Therefore, the fear of a likely loss will prompt them to take specific political pressures to sustain a given program (Higgs, 2014).

The transitional gains trap also provides a better understanding of the sustainability of various government social programs, including taxpayer-subsidized health insurance. The initial group of beneficiaries benefits the most from the fact that it is still relatively small. However, when it turns out that subsidizing subsequent beneficiaries is becoming more and more costly, among others because of factors such as demographic changes, an ageing society or chronic diseases, the benefits achieved by subsequent generations of beneficiaries are beginning to disappear. However, other groups will continue to strive to maintain their privileges due to the previously incurred subsidizing expenditures of previous beneficiaries, and so on (this is the case of, e.g., the Medicare program).

A similar effect is also visible in the case of the insured in marketplaces/exchanges who, despite the government covering most of their expenses, must deal with rising premiums, higher and higher out-of-pocket payments, or a limited network of suppliers. Although their benefits are decreasing, some of them will be determined to keep these insurances due to previously incurred expenditures and (recently) granted privileges, even though such an attitude generates losses for other insured persons, taxpayers, or insurers.

Further actions of the Republicans

Despite the failure to repeal ObamaCare, the Republicans continued to take action to improve the situation of various groups of Americans. It is worth pointing here to President Trump's order (decree) of October 2017 which would allow, among others, the creation of the so-called association health plans (AHPs). These plans would allow small employers and other smaller groups to merge into large groups of insured employers so that they can obtain better insurance conditions, as is the case with larger employers offering their employees lower premiums and broader insurance by spreading risk and administrative costs. Additionally, APPs could offer narrower coverage, be exempt from ObamaCare requirements or state laws (as with self-insurance plans) and operate across their borders. The inability to set higher premiums, for example, for ill people, was to be maintained, but such companies would then set relatively higher premiums for all their employees (Whitehouse.gov, 2017).

This was intended to support smaller companies and their employees who did not have the opportunity to merge into larger risk groups. However, this order encountered legal problems. In March 2019, the US District Court for the District of Columbia ruled that AHPs assumptions were not as planned because groups and entities without a genuine community of interests could not be covered by joint insurance. According to the Court, this means that AHP cannot be treated as a group health plan under the ERISA Act, which was the intention of the Department of Labour seeking to implement the President's order (Keith, 2019).

The same order also includes plans to create short-term limited duration insurance (STLDI) and health reimbursement arrangements (HRAs). STLDI was to be exempt from many ObamaCare regulations and provide a cheaper alternative to insurance on marketplaces/exchanges. This was to facilitate the conclusion of short-term insurance, for example, by people who cannot obtain health insurance at their workplace. In turn, the HRA was to facilitate the employee's retention of their previous insurance when resigning from work in a given company or when moving from one company to another (Whitehouse.gov, 2017).

It is also worth mentioning the presidential proclamation of October 2019, which (from November of the same year) required the immigrants to prove (within 30 days of their entry into the USA) that they have approved health insurance or financial resources intended to cover predictable medical expenses. Such approved insurance may be, for example, insurance concluded by the employer or other private insurance such as: short-term insurance, travel, or catastrophic insurance (with a high deductible, etc.). In turn, subsidized insurance contracted by marketplaces/exchanges or Medicaid insurance is not accepted. The new requirement mainly concerns immigrants with their families, but does not apply to refugees, asylum seekers, or certain other groups (KFF, 2019).

According to the official website of the White House, the purpose of these regulations is to limit the expenses incurred by suppliers (e.g., hospitals) that are associated with providing medical services to the uninsured. These expenses are often not compensated by the beneficiaries themselves and, thus, lead to higher taxes, premiums, or service charges. It is also pointed out that the uninsured often, in unjustified cases, use ambulance services. It is estimated that the total amount of unrecovered expenses allocated to the uninsured was on average about $35 billion in each of the last 10 years, and their average amount for each hospital is $7 million (Whitehouse.gov, 2019).

In this context, however, it is worth emphasizing that the situation is primarily the result of earlier regulations requiring hospital emergency departments to accept all people who report to them (EMTALA), restrictions on competition between hospitals (CON) or many state regulations that make health insurance not affordable, especially for people with lower incomes. In addition, the problem of the uninsured immigrants affects people staying in the USA illegally to a greater extent than those who are documented. Therefore, these requirements do not necessarily contribute to a significant improvement in the situation. They may increase the awareness of people coming to the USA (e.g., about the purchase of appropriate health insurance) but, above all, they should be supported by significant deregulation of the market, which would lead to a decrease in the prices of insurance or hospital services.

Other proposed changes

Representatives of the Democratic Party, in addition to proposals to expand support for the insured on marketplaces/exchanges or to introduce public options, also proposed more radical changes consisting in the creation of a single-payer system. These postulates became known as *Medicare for All,* and their main advocate was Senator Bernie Sanders.

The key tenets of this plan focused on creating government health insurance covering all Americans, providing them with comprehensive and unpaid medical services. Medicare for All would abolish the provider networks that currently apply to private insurance, insurance premiums, direct spending (including deductibles), and so on. In addition, the scope of the Medicare program was to be expanded to include services such as dentistry, vision and hearing treatment, long-term home care, and treatment of mental illnesses, and direct expenditure on the purchase of drugs would be limited to $200 per year (Berniesanders.com).

The main reasons for introducing such solutions are: 30 million people without insurance, rising direct spending on insurance, the world's highest per capita health care spending, worse health outcomes and infant mortality compared to other countries (Berniesanders.com).

However, all these problems have been thoroughly discussed in the previous parts of this chapter, and they are not the result of market failure but of government interventionism, a specific lifestyle of the population (including their eating habits) or accepted definitions, as is the case with statistics on infant mortality.

One of the arguments in favour of Medicare for All was to be lower administrative costs generated by Medicare compared to private insurance. Medicare for All would, therefore, allow for additional savings in the scale of the whole country that were to be used, among others, for additional medical services. However, this was a percentage view of the ratio of administrative costs to total Medicare costs, not their lower nominal amount, which only built a misleading picture of the situation. The Medicare program, due to the older insured persons, has much higher costs per beneficiary, which led to a reduction in the share of administrative costs. Moreover, a single-payer system would lead to an increase in rules, regulations, bureaucracy and, thus, to even higher costs of this kind.

In the discussion on the legitimacy of introducing Medicare for All, it should also be noted that no such system existing in other countries leads to a decrease in costs in health care, and an additional effect of its introduction is usually to ration access to health care. This is not the result of mismanagement or insufficient funds, but a structural disadvantage of this type of solution occurring in many developed countries such as Canada, the United Kingdom, Sweden, Norway, or Spain.

The entry into force of Medicare for All would also mean a tax increase. In 2020, the Committee for a Responsible Federal Budget published updated forecasts of the amount of expenditure on this type of program. They showed that the proposed solutions would increase federal spending from $25 billion to $35 billion over 10 years. Tax increases would, therefore, be necessary to finance these additional expenditures. For instance, to raise an additional $30 billion, the payroll tax alone would have to increase from 15.3% to 32%. Another solution could be, for example, the establishment of a new federal value added tax (VAT) of 42%. Therefore, to distribute the costs appropriately, the government could also decide to raise several different taxes and introduce new levies, as was the case with ObamaCare (Committee for a Responsible Federal Budget, 2020).

However, the most radical consequence of introducing this type of a solution would be likely deprivation of Americans of their private insurance, especially those concluded by the employer. Despite the various problems faced by the health insurance market, many of them would not support this idea, seeing problems with the government-created marketplaces/exchanges. This is one of the reasons why the Democrats decided on less radical and controversial solutions in the form of increasing funds for the goals implemented through ObamaCare, which was included in the election campaign of Joe Biden – their candidate for the office of president of the USA during the 2020 election.

Nonetheless, this does not mean that the creation of a single-payer system is impossible. Avik Roy, president of the Foundation for Research on Equal Opportunity and a former Republican adviser, points to the ongoing process of weakening of the private insurance – this time through *public options*, that is, government insurance designed to be cheaper competition for private ones. The public options proposed by the Democrats are supposed to be cheaper than employer insurance thanks to a lower reimbursement rate paid to hospitals and other providers. It would remain the same as in the case of Medicare, which is about 2.4 times lower than private insurance – relatively higher rates for the latter are mainly due to the monopoly that hospitals have on a given market (Roy, 2019).

This is not the first attempt to introduce such solutions. The Democrats wanted to introduce public options as early as 2010 through a standard legislative process requiring a minimum of 60 votes in the Senate. In the end, they received 58 votes. Roy believes that next time they can make such an attempt through an accelerated process (reconciliation) requiring a simple majority of votes. In addition, public options have a chance to be positively evaluated by Congress as a solution to reduce the deficit because their lower premiums would at the same time lead to lower tax credits compared to private insurance or those concluded on marketplaces/exchanges (Roy, 2019).

Assessment of the legitimacy of the introduction of ObamaCare and proposals for its further modifications

The effects of ObamaCare and the future of the US health care system

Economists of the Austrian School point out the importance of the structure of production in the process of managing scarce goods to improve the well-being of society. In the context of health systems, the structure of financing access to medical services is also of no less importance. Government interventions can significantly disrupt this structure and, thus, hinder their rational production and consumption.

Many Americans are directly experiencing these problems, for example, through limited supplier networks, rising insurance premiums and direct spending, and limited opportunities to purchase medical services in a form other than insurance. Despite this, many of them are convinced that these problems are the result of market failure, for example, because of the prevalence of private health insurance contracted by the employer, or the lack of a single-payer system covering all Americans. Some of them openly support individual political options promising to improve the situation by undertaking further interventions in this area.

Interestingly, statistics cited by the American Enterprise Institute (AEI) indicate that Americans' views on the functioning of their health system have not changed significantly for almost four decades, despite successive government interventions. For instance, in 1982, only 19% of respondents claimed that the system was functioning properly and that minor changes were needed, and in 2018 this percentage fell to 16%. Over the years, most respondents shared the opinion that there were several good elements in the American system, but fundamental changes were needed (47% in 1982 vs 52% in 2018). On the other hand, almost a third said that the system had many drawbacks, and a complete reconstruction was needed (28% in 1982 vs 31% in 2018) (American Enterprise Institute, 2019). Thus, these are only slight differences.

In its report, the AEI also presented Gallup research (November 2018) on health care costs in the USA. Not surprisingly, only 20% of respondents were generally satisfied with their costs compared to 79% of dissatisfied. In addition, 57% said it was up to the federal government to take action to ensure that all Americans had health insurance, while 42% did not see it as a task for the federal authorities. However, subsequent studies of this institution (December 2018) showed that support for the health care system led by the federal authorities was expressed only by the 40% of respondents, while 57% were inclined towards a system based mainly on private health insurance. In this respect, opinion polls can vary significantly. For instance, according to a FOX News poll (August 2018), 46% of those surveyed supported switching to a single-payer system called Medicare for All, 31% were against it, and 23% had no opinion. Yet another study by CBS News (October 2018) found that 65% of respondents were in favour of the proposal to offer federally administered health insurance to everyone, and 30% were against it (American Enterprise Institute, 2019).

These types of survey are an interesting tool for analysing social moods on a given topic. However, they cannot be used to confirm or refute economic claims or prove the correctness of the economic policy pursued or planned by the government. Respondents do not bear the direct costs or consequences of their answers. Many of them are also not aware of the real effects of the entry into force of the ideas they support at a given moment.

The latter issue is well illustrated by a 2019 study conducted by the Kaiser Family Foundation. They show a significant change in support for the idea of creating Medicare for All, depending on the possible consequences (Figure 4.1).

While the guarantee of providing insurance for all Americans, eliminating insurance premiums and reducing direct spending is supported by 71% and 67% of respondents, respectively, support for the creation of Medicare for All is significantly declining (to 37%) when it turns out that it can simultaneously lead to a tax increase or the elimination of private insurers and insurance. This idea has even less support among respondents (26%) when one of its consequences is given as an increase in waiting time for examinations and treatment. It should also be emphasized that such universal insurance would be difficult to maintain the Medicare standard. This name is deliberately used by politicians

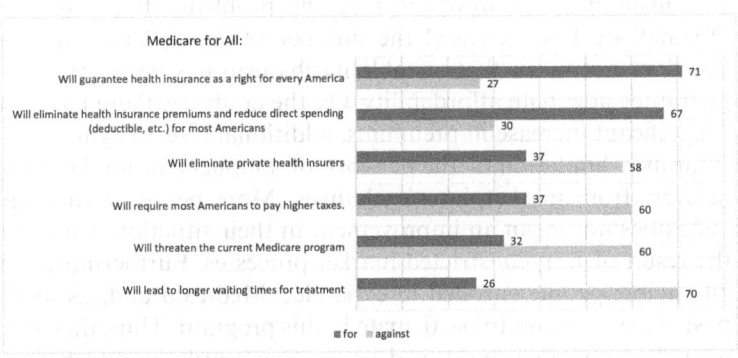

Figure 4.1 Change in support for the creation of Medicare for All in view of its possible impact on the current health system (in per cent)

Source: Own study, based on: KFF, 2020.

because Americans may associate it well in contrast to, for example, Medicaid. Indeed, trying to convince the public about Medicaid for All would not be so easy anymore due to the lower quality of services provided, and so on, which some voters may pay attention to.

Medicare for All is an obvious step towards perpetuating an inadequate funding structure that would only further exacerbate the existing problems. The same was true of ObamaCare. However, this should not come as a surprise, as the same interventionist measures were used as in the past. The sheer fact of having insurance will not solve problems with the availability of medical services because a lot depends on the age or health of the insured. Insurance will not work as a suitable tool for financing access to routine benefits, and so on. In addition, it is intended mainly for healthy people who have not yet experienced adverse events such as illness or accident. In other words, the insurance institution has limited ability to meet all the health needs of society. The advantage of non-constricted market processes is an appropriate (rational) structure of financing access to such benefits. Insurance plays an important role, as do direct payments, but this also requires a lack of intervention on the supply side. The government cannot interfere in the process of educating doctors or building new medical facilities, as it does in the USA.

Policymakers think that government or subsidized private insurance will solve most of the problems. It is true that ObamaCare has increased the number of insured persons, but this does not mean that a stable mechanism has been created to guarantee adequate affordability. On the contrary, there has been a significant increase in premiums, additional direct payments for insurance, limitation of the network of suppliers, or loud exits of insurers from marketplaces/exchanges. More people with insurance does not mean an improvement in their situation if it is not the result of non-constricted market processes. Furthermore, not all eligible people enrolled in expanded Medicaid and, as in the past, were reluctant to participate in this program. Thus, they were formally uninsured, but this does not necessarily have to be seen as a problem.

According to the US Census Bureau, the number of the uninsured (throughout the whole year) in 2013 amounted to 42 million people, which accounted for 13.4% of the entire US population

(Smith & Medalia, 2014, p. 2). In 2019, this number fell to 26 million uninsured (8% of the population). Some of the new insured – about 10 million – gained access to insurance through subsidized marketplaces/exchanges (Keisler-Starkey & Bunch, 2020, p. 5). Others took advantage of Medicaid's expansion, so it was another part of society dependent on the government. Still, the 26 million people without insurance in some way demonstrate the ineffectiveness of ObamaCare, and it is hard to expect this to improve, even under Democrats. However, this is not the result of reducing the penalty for lack of insurance to zero, or lack of adequate support for insurers, as widespread problems were already visible with attracting enough insured in multiple states. In turn, the reluctance to cover the losses of insurers was the result of, on the one hand, the constantly growing spending in the first years of ObamaCare and, on the other hand, President Obama's lack of adequate funds for these purposes.

Interestingly, the requirement to have health insurance and the new regulations covering employers, introduced by ObamaCare, have also contributed to a change in the interpretation of sources of spending (private-public) on health care by some institutions. For instance, the OECD in its recent *Health at a Glance* reports informs that, since the introduction of ObamaCare in 2014, the share of public spending has increased significantly, among other things, due to the obligation to have insurance. Since 2014, private health insurance concluded individually (e.g., on marketplaces/exchanges) and by the employer has been classified as public expenditure, as they operate under a compulsory insurance system, as is the case in, for example, Switzerland or the Netherlands (OECD, 2019, p. 150). That is why the share of this type of spending in the USA has been so high for several years. In 2019, it amounted to about 85% of total expenditure compared to 48% in 2013 (Figure 4.2).

The changes in the OECD's classification of expenditure data, although not directly aimed at this, illustrate the progressive interventionism in the USA. However, the authors of the report emphasize that due to the limited possibilities of more accurate data measurement, other private voluntary insurances (OECD, 2019, p. 150) have been added to the (mandatory and already public) insurance concluded by the employer, even their exclusion would not result in a significant reduction in the share of public expenditure, that is, it would not be close to the 2013 level again.

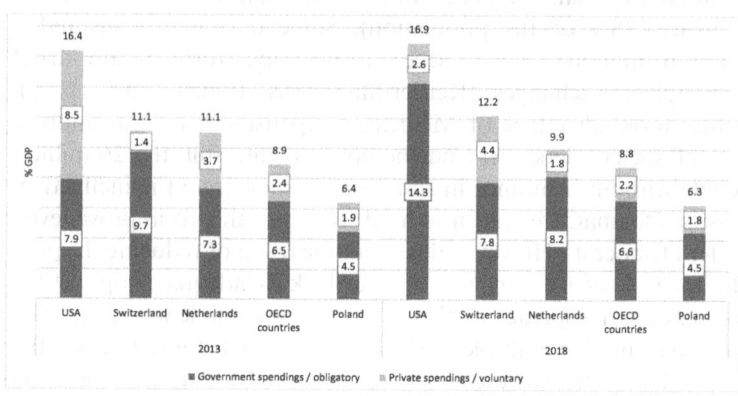

Figure 4.2 The share of health care spending in the USA by source and selected countries (as a percentage of GDP)

Source: Own study, based on: OECD, 2019, p. 153; OECD, 2015, p. 167.

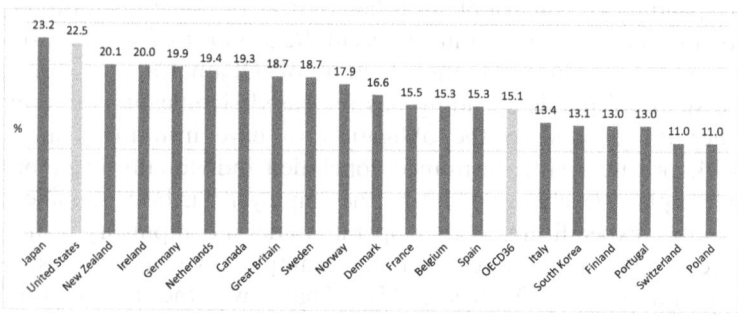

Figure 4.3 Public health care spending as a percentage of total government spending (in per cent)

Source: Own study, based on: OECD, 2019, p. 159.

However, even without considering mandatory and voluntary private insurance, there is a greater involvement of public funds. The OECD reports that in 2017, health care spending from public sources accounted for 22.5% of total government spending, which, after Japan, was the second highest record in the world (Figure 4.3). For comparison, in 2013 this percentage was 20%, which at that time placed the USA in the 4th position. On the other hand, spending from public sources (excluding private insurance, etc.) on health care in 2017 in the USA accounted for only 50% of total expenditure, which still should be considered significant (OECD, 2019, p. 159). At the same time, the vast and ever-expanding regulatory sphere covering the remaining half of private spending must not be forgotten. This is one of the reasons why the OECD's reclassification, related to the obligation to have health insurance, may easily draw the observers' attention to the issue of rethinking the allegedly market model of the American system.

Market-based alternative

Interventionism in US health care is focused, among other things, on exposing the growing role of third-party payers, whether by creating government insurance or by supporting quasi-private markets with private entities but operating based on several government guidelines. This leads to an increased demand for health insurance and a reduction in the share of direct payments. Such a distorted financing structure significantly contributes to the increase in spending (and costs) on medical services and discourages cost-effective action on the part of consumers and suppliers (Figure 4.4).

Therefore, Figure 4.1 can be considered a visual quintessence of the problems of the American health system. Many Americans perceive insurance as a solution to the problem of constantly growing costs, while not noticing that their exposure is the main cause of the problem and not its solution. Hence, there are constant tendencies to expand the scope of such insurance or their appropriate regulations, for example, guaranteeing protection for people with a higher health risk. In turn, lack of insurance is perceived as an undesirable situation that can cause significant financial and health problems. In part, these concerns are understandable. It should be stressed, however, that the unpopularity of direct payments also has its roots in strong supply-side regulations which artificially restrict market competition and grant monopoly privileges to certain entities.

As a real solution to these problems, one should indicate the market health care system with its dynamic and diversified structure of financing health services which does not favour one

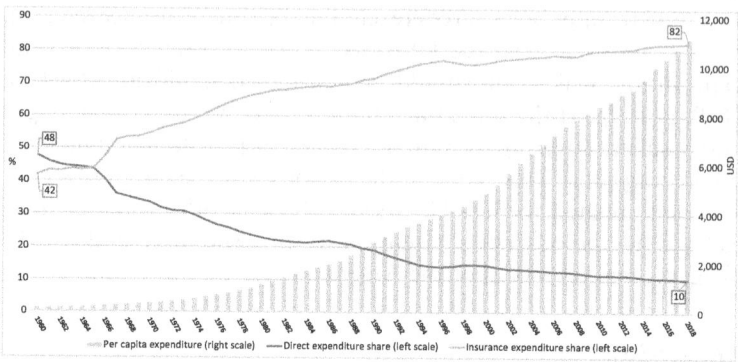

Figure 4.4 Change in the share of individual types of health care expenditure (in per cent) in total expenditure and per capita expenditure in 1960–2018

Note: Expenditure on health insurance includes expenditure on: (1) private insurance; (2) Medicare, Medicaid, CHIP public insurance; (3) other public expenditure related to the third-party payer and other public programmes, including but not limited to: marketplaces/exchanges subsidies and other expenditure (e.g., state and local grants, etc.).

Source: Own study, based on: Centers for Medicare and Medicaid Services.

pre-selected form (e.g., insurance), but thus allows for the formation of a specific spontaneous order (Figure 4.5).

In this system, insurance still plays an important role. However, this institution is not responsible for financing access to most of the benefits. Thanks to this, the financing of certain less expensive or routine services can be *taken over,* for example, by medical networks offering subscriptions, doctors and hospitals accepting direct payments or charitable institutions, which are responsible for correcting various problems with adjustments that may occur in the basic structure. In the real economy there will always be uncertainty, people will make mistakes, and so on. Such a system cannot be effectively designed in advance, hence the important role of charitable institutions. Furthermore, this system would be highly competitive, and the importance of the different forms of financing could (to some extent) be complemented and changed over time. For instance, competition between suppliers, along with technological progress, would lead to successive reductions in costs and prices. Thanks to better affordability, having a subscription or

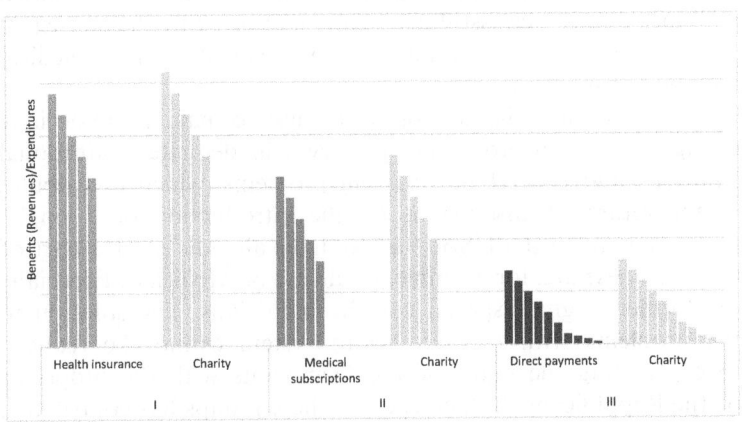

Figure 4.5 Benefits achieved by consumers of medical services in relation to the expenses incurred according to individual forms of financing accessed to these benefits

Source: Own study.

insurance would not have to be as necessary as it is now. Awareness of a healthy lifestyle and social responsibility for those in need would also increase.

Such a system would also mean an effective barrier against intervention in other areas of the economy. For instance, planned tax increases could be interpreted as indirectly limiting the possibility of private financing of access to medical services, and so on. Therefore, the issue of introducing a market health system cannot be considered in isolation from the entire economy because both areas somehow complement each other. The market health system operates based on sovereign decisions and private savings of consumers. Its success may also be a determinant for greater liberalization of other areas of the economy, for example, the pension system, and so on.

In conclusion, it is worth emphasizing that to create such a system, more decisive and courageous actions must be taken, which may be met with the dissatisfaction of a part of public opinion. From an economic point of view, however, they are necessary to provide the society with more affordable medical services. Importantly, these activities must include both the demand and the and supply side. Deregulation of the health insurance market will not be fully successful if it is not supported by the consistent abolition of regulations limiting the number of doctors, medical facilities, or medicines.

In this context, the lack of willingness to make more decisive changes in a dangerous way preserves inadequate institutional solutions and exacerbates existing problems, which contributes to the return of discussions on the introduction of a single-payer system. In the USA, such systems already cover a part of society. These are, for example, Medicare or Medicaid. Especially the former is given special care by politicians. The solution to the problems with the US health system cannot be reduced to contrasting the plans of the Democrats with the proposals of the Republicans. In fact, each of these groups has contributed to expanding the government's influence in this area of the economy. The Democrats introduced Medicare, Medicaid, and ObamaCare. The Republicans also have a significant track record in this regard. One can mention here President Ronald Reagan, who signed the EMTALA Act imposing many new regulations on hospitals; President George W. Bush extending Medicare to subsidize the insured when buying prescription drugs (Part D, Medicare); or another politician of this party – Mitt Romney – who is one of the main initiators of compulsory insurance in the state of Massachusetts. In the end, the Republicans were also unable to (at least partially) repeal ObamaCare. Despite their concrete efforts directed to this goal, one should not lose sight of the whole picture of the American health system, which had been increasingly regulated for many decades before ObamaCare. As interventionism continues, there is a growing need for more decisive solutions that prioritize choice rather than coercion. More compromise-based solutions will not bring the expected results and will, thus, provoke further interventions.

Notes

1 Hence the name *skinny repeal*, as it is known.
2 For more on this topic, see: Tullock, 1975, pp. 671–678.

References

American Enterprise Institute (2019). AEI Political Report: The polls on the past and future of health care reform, www.aei.org/wp-content/uplo ads/2019/03/Political-Report-March-2019.pdf (accessed: 3.11.2020).

Berniesanders.com (n. d.). Health care as a human right – Medicare for All, https://berniesanders.com/issues/medicare-for-all/ (accessed: 27.10.2020).

Centers for Medicare and Medicaid Services (n.d.). National health expenditures by type of service and source of funds, CY 1960–2018, www.cms.gov/Research-Statistics-Data-and-Systems/Statistics-Trends-and-Reports/NationalHealthExpendData/NationalHealthAccount sHistorical (accessed: 11.10.2020).

Committee for a Responsible Federal Budget (2020). Choices for financing Medicare for All, www.crfb.org/papers/choices-financing-medic are-all (accessed: 27.10.2020).

Custer, B. (2016). Sadly, one does not simply repeal ObamaCare, https://fee.org/articles/sadly-one-does-not-simply-repeal-obamacare/?utm_source=zapier&utm_medium=facebook (accessed: 15.10.2020).

Galles, G. (2018). The legal gymnastics behind ObamaCare, https://mises.org/wire/legal-gymnastics-behind-obamacare (accessed: 14.10.2020).

Glassman, J. K. (2020). Drug price controls endanger seniors, www.nationalreview.com/2020/10/drug-price-controls-endanger-seniors/ (accessed: 15.10.2020).

Goodman, J. C. (2018). Why is ObamaCare more popular than the GOP tax cuts? www.forbes.com/sites/johngoodman/2018/08/27/why-is-obamacare-more-popular-than-the-gop-tax-cuts/#5b6555d63bbb (accessed: 22.10.2020).

Higgs, R. (2014). Gordon Tullock and the transitional gains trap, https://blog.independent.org/2014/11/06/gordon-tullock-and-the-transitional-gains-trap/ (accessed: 23.10.2020).

Keisler-Starkey, K., & Bunch, L. N. (2020). *Health insurance coverage in the United States: 2019*. US Census Bureau.

Keith, K. (2019). Court invalidates rule on association health plans, www.healthaffairs.org/do/10.1377/hblog20190329.393236/full/ (accessed: 26.10.2020).

KFF (Kaiser Family Foundation) (2017). Summary of the Health Care Freedom Act, http://files.kff.org/attachment/Summary-of-the-Health-Care-Freedom-Act (accessed: 21.10.2020).

KFF (Kaiser Family Foundation) (2019). President Trump's proclamation suspending entry for immigrants without health coverage, www.kff.org/racial-equity-and-health-policy/fact-sheet/president-trumps-proclamation-suspending-entry-for-immigrants-without-health-cover age/ (accessed: 26.10.2020).

KFF (Kaiser Family Foundation) (2020). Public opinion on single-payer, national health plans, and expanding access to Medicare coverage, www.kff.org/slideshow/public-opinion-on-single-payer-national-hea lth-plans-and-expanding-access-to-medicare-coverage/ (accessed: 3.11.2020).

Levitt, L. (2020). Trump vs Biden on health care, https://jamanetwork. com/channels/health-forum/fullarticle/2770427?fbclid=IwAR2I84_ xGcZPBflrhCFm65OWQ8TTkVpxikYU1B3UO1UW_GZxGqOR tOTLBX4 (accessed: 15.10.2020).

McAuliff, M. (2017). McCain votes No, derails 'skinny repeal' in mara-thon session, https://khn.org/news/mccain-votes-no-derails-skinny-rep eal-in-marathon-session/ (accessed: 21.10.2020).

OECD (2015). *Health at a glance 2015: OECD indicators.* OECD Publishing.

OECD (2019). *Health at a glance 2019: OECD indicators.* OECD Publishing.

Roy, A. (2019). To stop socialized medicine, expand individual choice, www.nationalreview.com/2019/05/stop-socialized-medicine-expand-individual-choice/ (accessed: 28.10.2020).

Scott, D., & Kliff, S. (2017). Why ObamaCare repeal failed, www.vox. com/policy-and-politics/2017/7/31/16055960/why-obamacare-repeal-failed (accessed: 21.10.2020).

Smith, J. C., & Medalia, C. (2014). *Health insurance coverage in the United States: 2013.* Census Bureau.

Tucker, J. (2016). The election became a referendum on ObamaCare, https://fee.org/articles/the-election-turned-on-obamacare/?utm_sou rce=zapier&utm_medium=facebook (accessed: 15.10.2020).

Tullock, G. (1975). 'The transitional gains trap', *Bell Journal of Economics,* 2: 671–678.

The United States Senate Republican Policy Committee (2017). The American Health Care Act of 2017, www.rpc.senate.gov/policy-papers/ the-american-health-care-act-of-2017 (accessed: 21.10.2020).

Whitehouse.gov (2017). Presidential executive order promoting healthcare choice and competition across the United States, www.whitehouse.gov/ presidential-actions/presidential-executive-order-promoting-healthc are-choice-competition-across-united-states/ (26.10.2020).

Whitehouse.gov (2019). Presidential proclamation on the suspension of entry of immigrants who will financially burden the United States healthcare system, www.whitehouse.gov/presidential-actions/president ial-proclamation-suspension-entry-immigrants-will-financially-bur den-united-states-healthcare-system/ (accessed: 26.10.2020).

Summary

The presentation of the ObamaCare from the economics perspective has demonstrated that an appropriate financing structure for access to medical services is crucial. The market structure is not fixed and may be subject to some changes. Most of the society does not have to be covered by insurance. This is because this institution has limited possibilities to effectively meet the health needs of people with higher health risks or to finance access to routine services. Therefore, it should be supplemented by alternative forms such as direct payments. It also requires far-reaching changes and deregulation on the supply side, which will contribute to greater competition and affect more rational consumption of medical services.

The analysis conducted in this book showed that a significant increase in costs and expenses or difficulties in buying health insurance result from extensive interventionism. The health insurance market is particularly important here. Many government interventions, even before ObamaCare, made it impossible for insurance to perform its function properly. Insurers do not have adequate freedom in the process of risk calculation. Another negative consequence of this situation is the marginalization of direct payments. Paradoxically, this may make it difficult to make the necessary changes, as Americans directly bear only a fraction of the cost.

Meanwhile, the federal and state governments have consistently introduced new regulations over many decades to address these problems. However, they did not lead to their solution but to their deepening. It can also lead to the erroneous conclusion that they are the result of the actions of market processes, and improving the situation requires even more decisive action. Consequently, the

American system is subject to more and more regulations, more and more people are dependent on government support, and so on.

Recent major changes in the form of ObamaCare have also contributed to this unfavourable process. They have only led to an increase in premiums, direct payments (e.g., deductibles), or public expenditure. One should also add loud exits of insurers, a smaller number of suppliers or their limited networks. Also, the number of the insured on the marketplaces/exchanges is not as large as expected and, in addition, in recent years it has started to decrease. All these factors do not prove an improvement in access to medical services, and their culmination has turned out to be a spiral of affordability which covered the whole country and did not concern a single case, that is, a specific health plan.

The regulations introduced by ObamaCare did not differ significantly from those introduced in the past. Thus, they could not improve the situation. In fact, the government has limited possibilities to apply new solutions because these ultimately boil down to even more interventions. When previous interventions do not produce the expected results, others of even greater scope are proposed. Such actions consistently direct the American health system towards a single-payer system. Institutional conditions mean that this path leads through further weakening and regulating the private health insurance market. This is one of the reasons why it is proposed to extend financial support (e.g., in the form of reliefs or reduction of direct expenses) to a larger number of people insured on the marketplaces/exchanges, or to introduce the so-called public options to be an alternative to insurance concluded by the employer.

However, the situation will be improved by reverse actions consisting in deregulation of the health insurance market and other areas of the American system, which will also lead to the development of alternative forms of financing access to medical services and relieve the burden on insurers and the insured.

Finally, it is also worth indicating potential directions for further research in the topic discussed. One of them may be the question of how the deregulation of the entire system could be carried out, that is, its marketization. These issues may cover individual areas such as the insurance market, the medicines market, hospitals, and so on. Another potential issue to examine is to take a closer look at the reasons why private entities (e.g., insurers) decide to cooperate with the government, and investigate the impact of these decisions on their further functioning. The example of marketplaces/ exchanges shows that this was a big mistake of insurers. Such actions should also not be equated with non-constricted market processes. Private entities operating within the framework of an increasing number of regulations are not a free market, and this should not be forgotten.

Index